2 WEEK LOAN

This item is to be returned to the library on or before the last date stamped below.

WITHDRAWN

Keighley College

To renew telephone 01535 685010

library@leedscitycollege.ac.uk

RHONDA

VERTICAL

Vegetables
& Fruit

CREATIVE
GARDENING TECHNIQUES
for
GROWING UP
IN SMALL SPACES

Storey Publishing

The mission of Storey Publishing is to serve our customers by
publishing practical information that encourages
personal independence in harmony with the environment.

Edited by Gwen Steege, Carleen Madigan, and Lisa H. Hiley
Art direction by Jessica Armstrong
Book design and text production by Michael Vrana/Black Eye Design Inc.
Illustrations by © Kathryn Rathke
Indexed by Christine R. Lindemer, Boston Road Communications

Storey Publishing
210 MASS MoCA Way
North Adams, MA 01247
www.storey.com

Printed in the United States by Versa Press
10 9 8 7 6 5 4 3 2 1

LIBRARY OF CONGRESS CATALOGING-IN-PUBLICATION DATA

Hart, Rhonda Massingham, 1959–
  Vertical vegetables and fruit / by Rhonda Massingham Hart.
    p. cm.
  Includes index.
  First ed. published as: Trellising.
  ISBN 978-1-60342-998-6 (pbk. : alk. paper)
  1. Vertical gardening. 2. Trellises. I. Title.
SB463.5.M37 2012
631.5'46—dc23
                          2011024851

To my beautiful, spectacular, brilliant daughter,
Kaelah, and my handsome, amazing, awesome son,
Lance — the absolute joys of my life.

Love you, Mombo

ACKNOWLEDGMENTS

I hope you read this. It's the part of a book in which the grateful author gets to thank "all the little people" who helped. I'm not that deluded. In reality, I barely helped the people who actually did the work. I just wrote the thing. The folks who made it readable, fun to look at, and small enough to carry (not to mention print it, bind it, and haul it off to market) are the ones who should get the real credit.

So here's to the real stars of the show. Publisher Pam Art came up with idea in the first place. We all owe her our thanks. Gwen Steege and Carleen Madigan got the ball rolling. Send them roses. Jessica Richard had the job of herding feral cats in the forms of a writer, business contracts, and other grown-up stuff. There should a medal for that, or at least therapy. Jessica Armstrong wrangled Michel Vrana, the intuitive and gifted graphic designer. They both deserve tremendous credit; someone should take them out to dinner — but maybe not together. Ilona Sherratt oversaw the images I sent, along with those that actually made it into the book; chocolates to her. Kathryn Rathke, the illustrator, created the dead-on perfect illustrations you're about to see, on a tight deadline, no less. Champagne perhaps? And Lisa Hiley knitted the whole works together as project editor; roses, dinner, chocolates, *and* champagne to her!

v

Contents

Introduction vii

PART I
THE WHYS, WHATS, AND HOW-TOS OF MAKING FOOD GROW UP

Chapter 1 | It's Time to Grow Up! 2
Chapter 2 | Making the Most of Materials 11
Chapter 3 | Traditional Techniques: Tepees and Trellises 19
Chapter 4 | Not-So-Traditional Tricks:
Hanging, Stacking, Towering, and More 31

PART II
VERTICAL ANNUAL VINES

Chapter 5 | Beans 48
Chapter 6 | Peas 56
Chapter 7 | Tomatoes 61
Chapter 8 | Cucumbers 72
Chapter 9 | Squash and Gourds 78
Chapter 10 | Melons 86
Chapter 11 | Sweet Potatoes 97

PART III
FINE PERENNIAL FRUITS

Chapter 12 | Blackberries 104
Chapter 13 | Raspberries 110
Chapter 14 | Strawberries 117
Chapter 15 | Grapes 123
Chapter 16 | Kiwis 132
Chapter 17 | The Essentials of Espalier 138

Appendix 1 | A Note on Recommended Varieties 151
Appendix 2 | Direct Seeding 154
Appendix 3 | Growing Your Own Seedlings 155
Appendix 4 | Hardening Off Tender Transplants 157

Resources for Gardeners 158
Index 163

Introduction

W e've all seen them. Those gorgeous, elaborate examples of trellised plants beckon, even if only from the pages of the latest garden magazine or website. Images of billowing clouds of climbing roses, obediently outstretched arms of espaliered fruit trees, and cascading waves of wisteria reach from the pages to flirt with our imagination and tug at our envious hearts. Such visions of the gardener's devotion are surely beyond us, the Keepers of the Home Plot, so pressed for time, space, and available resources. Or are they?

True, creating these living works of art takes time and dedication, both things today's backyard gardener often finds in short supply. But the techniques that are used in achieving these glorious results can be put to good use by even the most harried of home growers. The results may be less dramatic with trellised beans or cucumbers than with ornamental flowers, but that depends entirely on one's perspective. Whether you trellis plants for fine art or fine harvests, one of the most appreciable results will be a less harried, less tired, more satisfied gardener!

The principles of trellising garden crops are few and simple. Climbing stems or vines are trained onto upright supports

Using cinder blocks is just one of many resourceful ways to create vertical space in your backyard, an existing garden, or even a deck or balcony.

either by means of their own climbing growth habits or by being tied in place. A support or trellis generally consists of standards or a frame, and plant supports. The trellis may be a permanent structure or a seasonal garden fixture.

Creative gardeners with limited space are always experimenting with ways to grow food up, and some of their solutions are nothing short of inspiring. While trellising remains the most common method of vertical crop production, this book offers other ideas for growing food in spaces you may have never thought possible, from potato towers to hanging baskets to wonderful walls of produce and more.

This book is about growing your own food in whatever space you have, whether it's a full garden, a strip of an alley, an apartment balcony, or just a windowsill. It's about taking a step toward self-sufficiency and healthy eating. It will show you the best materials to use and how to use them. Basic designs and plans for different types of trellises and which plants are most suited to them are covered. A gallery of some of the best candidates for trellising follows under headings for each specific crop along with suggestions of varieties to try.

A surprising variety of plants can be trained to grow up just about anywhere, anytime. Whereas training perennial vines to a trellis is a gradual process, single-season crops such as tomatoes, squash, and peas yield more immediate results. Best of all are the benefits that a vertical garden offers to both plant and gardener. Freeing up ground space, or making the most of a small plot, is just the beginning. Once you've seen how easy it can be, I'm sure you'll embrace and enjoy this upward trend and wonder why it took you so long to grow up!

PART I

The Whys, Whats, and How-tos

{ OF MAKING FOOD GROW UP }

O f all the clever techniques gardeners have devised for squeezing the very most from a patch of dirt, training a climbing — or at least pliable — vine up a support structure is one of the simplest yet most ingenious. The advantages, in case you need a little convincing that constructing a trellis or an A-frame is worth the effort, are varied and numerous, especially if you fear inadvertently inviting an Audrey II (the uncontrollable, man-eating vine from *Little Shop of Horrors*) into your garden. But the gist is that by allowing a vine to follow the sun, you will be richly rewarded with heavenly harvests.

Does the idea of a trip to the lumberyard to stock up on supplies fill you with dread? It needn't. Though arbors and pergolas can certainly be a part of training any trailing or vining plant to grow up, more modest materials are often just as suitable, and can be quite inexpensive or even free. The trick is in knowing how to use them.

Which brings us to the topic of constructing a support system. People often wonder, Isn't it a lot of work, and don't the structures look unsightly unless you spend a lot of money, and aren't there a lot of other good reasons to spare yourself the trouble? The answer to all of the above is, It's up to you. Trellises can be purchased ready-made and freestanding or fashioned from designs as simple or as complex as you choose.

Inexpensive doesn't have to look cheap, but even if it does, the state of the structure underneath matters little once a healthy vine obscures it with lush, beautiful foliage. And once you've experienced the rewards, you can decide for yourself whether they were worth the extra effort — if indeed it feels like any extra effort after all.

CHAPTER 1

IT'S TIME TO

GROW

UP!

Don't have room for sprawling pumpkin vines? Settling for plain old bush beans instead of the variety of colors, textures, and tastes available with old-fashioned pole beans? Put off by the idea of tripping through tangled masses of space-hogging vines of cucumbers, melons, or rambling squash?

Fear not — you can free yourself to grow whatever your heart desires. No matter how little space you have in your garden, chances are that you have been totally over-looking most of your available growing area — that often neglected vertical space.

MAXIMIZE YOUR SPACE

Every square foot of garden space comes with a bonus 6 cubic feet or more of usable grow-ing space above it. The actual ground space taken up by any one vine may be reduced to just a couple of square inches. Training your plants upward lets you squeeze a lot more life into a small patch of earth than vines trailing all over the ground would ever allow, so you can grow more of a favorite crop or experi-ment with something new and different.

Another benefit of vertical gardening is that some plants naturally take a liking to one another, and the best way to take advantage of your extra space is to fill it — if only tempo-rarily — with plants that grow well together. Quick-growing plants, such as lettuce, spinach, and radishes, make excellent filler beneath vining canopies or quick intermediary

With careful planning, you can grow several different crops in close proximity. Always be aware of the direction of the sun to make sure that taller plants don't shade those in the front row.

crops while the vines are getting started, provided of course, they are mutually amenable.

Pay Special Attention to the Soil

Squeezing a few more plants into the same plot of earth requires extra effort on the part of your garden plot and a little more attention to the health of the soil on your part. The increased nutritional demands of additional plants will drain more of the soil's available nutrients.

Organic practices — such as composting, growing and tilling under green manure crops, top-dressing with seasoned animal manures, or treating growing plants to an occasional cup of fish emulsion — replace the

GROW ORGANIC!

According to the USDA's most recent list, the top offenders in the pesticide-residue wars are celery, peaches, strawberries, apples, domestic blueberries, nectarines, sweet bell peppers, spinach (also kale and collard greens), cherries, potatoes, imported grapes, and lettuce.

You can always buy organic produce at the grocery store and shop the local farmers market, but most of these crops are easily grown in a backyard or even on a deck, so there's no reason not to supplement your shopping with some homegrown produce that you know for a fact is completely free of residue.

extra nutrients used, increase the amount of organic matter in the soil, and improve its texture and drainage. Plants grown in soil rich in organic matter are also usually less vulnerable to soilborne pests.

LESS UPKEEP

Even though you may be utilizing every conceivable bit of your garden space to produce ground-greedy crops, there is another significant benefit to growing those same plants vertically: It makes a big difference in your workload. Less area available to produce competitive plant life (otherwise known as weeds) directly translates into less weeding.

Smaller spaces to dig, mulch, and clean up for winter mean less wear and tear on the gardener. Using less garden space also means spending less time doing all those gardening chores. You might even have time to use some of your newly freed-up valuable real estate for other things, like a hammock!

MADE IN THE SHADE

Sun-loving crops are often squeezed for space in small plots, but growing them up a trellis allows them to stretch out in the sun. The result is more surface area exposed to sunlight. But what about that little patch of shade created beneath those lounging vines?

It could provide just the spot for you to rest your weary gardening bones in the shade of a grape arbor or trellised blackberries or cherry tomatoes. Consider installing a well-deserved garden bench.

Many plants also appreciate a shaded spot in the plot. You could add a patch of salad greens, spinach, or a cole crop (anything in the cabbage family). Or you might provide a birdbath or a small pond to pamper garden guests such as birds, beneficial insects, and toads, which will in turn lend their appetites to your cause.

MORE REASONS TO GROW UP

If you're not already convinced, here are three more good reasons to grow food on the vertical rather than with those traditional earthbound methods: Plants grown vertically have access to more air and light, pest management is easier, and you typically will increase your yield.

Let There Be Light (and Air)

Not only does training your vines upward allow for more sunlight to reach those energy-gathering leaves, but it also allows for freer movement of the air surrounding the leaves. Better ventilation translates into healthier foliage.

SAVING SEEDS, SAVING CENTS

Here's a tactic that will increase the value of your humble plot, thus saving you money and, in a real sense, preserving some of the past. Most older trailing varieties of everything from beans to pumpkins are open-pollinated, meaning they set seed that will grow plants just like the parent plant. Most "new introductions" are hybrids: Either they won't set mature seed at all or their seeds will not grow true to the parent plants.

In a world of ever-increasing control of seed stock by corporations and ever-declining choices of mostly hybrid plants, saving your own seed from favorite heritage varieties is more than just good gardening practice — it's like growing your own little revolution.

An A-frame with a couple of narrow raised beds increases your growing space considerably. Wider beds provide space for a different crop in front of the vines, or use the shaded space between for a bed of spinach while the vines establish themselves.

Vines growing along the ground create a moist, still microenvironment underneath their canopy of overlapping leaves, which is perfect for many disease organisms and damaging fungi. Many of these diseases are spread by wind, splashing water, pest vectors, or physical contact as the gardener works around plants. Warm, wet conditions often encourage the rapid spread of disease.

Elevating the foliage effectively eliminates a prime source of contamination: ground contact. Also, it can significantly reduce a major cause of plant-to-plant transmission: moist, overlapping growth. Air circulates more freely among the raised vines and leaves and keeps their surfaces drier, which helps prevent diseases from starting or spreading.

Keep an Eagle Eye on Pests

Dozens of pests abound to terrorize our carefully tended crops. Many brazenly take advantage of a plant's growth habit and hide among the spreading foliage. Most thrive in the damp, shaded microclimate provided by those ground-hugging plants. Plants that ramble aimlessly about the garden offer nearly unlimited access because a great deal of their surface area is in contact with the soil. Pulling these errant stems off the ground and guiding them up vertical supports drastically reduces potential entry points.

Skybound vines are easier to inspect at a glance than their unkempt cousins, and bugs are easier to spot on orderly trained vines than on overlapping tangles of vegetation. Raising the vines off the ground makes looking for pests physically easier, too. Rather than hunching and bending and continually shoving wayward growth from your path, inspecting a neatly trained, trellised vine often requires little more than a quick nod of your head and a flick of a few leaves.

Trellised plants are not only easier to check for pests, but they are also more efficiently treated when invaders are spotted. Any sprays or dusts that you may need to apply can be administered more accurately, reducing the amount needed. And you eliminate the risk of accidentally stepping on and crushing vines or fruit.

Higher Plants, Higher Yields

Two separate strategies are at work here. First, although plant breeders are always striving for improvement in disease resistance, taste, and crop yields, in many cases old-time varieties consistently outperform the newcomers. Bush or compact varieties are generally the great-great-grandchildren of vining ancestors. The vining varieties of everything from peas and beans to tomatoes and squash are often genetically superior and produce more better-tasting fruit over a longer period of time than do their more compact cousins.

Second, even without overwhelming evidence from repeated research, it is not difficult to understand why a plant grown up a trellis will soon surpass an identical plant grown using conventional methods. What a privileged life it leads! Not only does it have the advantage of more sunshine and fewer pests, as described above, the trellised plant is also easier to water. It is further shielded from undue nutrient and light competition because it is easier to weed. With all of these advantages, how could it not produce higher yields!

RULES TO GROW BY

Garden crops really need only three things: sunlight, water, and soil. Everything else just boils down to making sure they can take advantage of those essential elements.

Rule № 1: Let the Sun Shine In

Situate crops so they get at least six hours of sunlight per day. Sun-deprived plants may survive, and even grow, but they will lack that healthy green color that photosynthesis imparts. They rarely flower or fruit and, if they do manage it, yield unsatisfactory produce that isn't worth your trouble.

Training plants to grow vertically increases the surface area exposed to sunlight. Just be sure to always position vertical support struc-

> Crops will grow bigger, better, faster, and more consistently with a properly timed supply of water to their roots.

tures to the north end of your space to avoid leaving other sun-loving plants in the dark.

Rule № 2: Water Wisely

Once upon a time we thought of water as an everlasting, abundant, unlimited resource. Just like passenger pigeons.

Overhead sprinklers, one of the most common methods of watering, are also the most inefficient and wasteful, especially on the broad leaves of plants such as squash and cucumbers. The wide leaves divert the spray from the root area of the plants and send it splashing off onto yet more leaves, wasting hundreds of gallons of water. Evaporation as the water sails from the sprinkler head also claims a fair amount of moisture.

Vines that are trained politely up a trellis are much easier to water without waste. The soil line near the stem of a plant is exposed so that water can penetrate to the roots. Any one of several efficient methods can be used.

NO MORE GROWING PAINS

Perspective is everything. Twenty years ago, when I wrote *Trellising,* I never thought twice about bending, yanking, shoveling, raking, and so on. These days, it sometimes hurts just to write about all that. I've noticed over the years that the more I train plants to grow up, the less aching (and complaining!) I do.

Though I'll talk later about styles of trellises, something to keep in mind is that your design options are totally unlimited. If you have a physical condition that limits your mobility, there is no rule that says your food source has to taunt you from ground level or mock you from above. Design your trellis system so that plants can be trained at a height that is comfortable for you to work at. Fruit or leaf thinning, insect and disease monitoring, and harvesting are a lot less stressful when done in a comfortable position.

An underground watering system can be as simple as a series of gallon jugs with a few holes punched in each, set in the ground at the same time your seedlings go in.

A drip irrigation system saves time, money, and water. As for the hassle of setup, have you ever tracked the time it takes to move sprinklers, drag and untangle hoses, fidget with settings and couplers, and then set it all up again?

Aqua spikes are tapered, 8-inch (20 cm) hollow spikes that fit on the end of 2-liter soda bottles. With the area around the roots cleared of vegetation, it's a snap to pop these into the ground, affix a filled bottle, and let the plants water themselves.

Make your own irrigation system by drilling or punching small holes in the bottom of a bucket, plastic milk jug, large-sized coffee can, or other suitable container. Bury the container near the vines when you transplant them; fill it periodically with water to provide steady moisture for growing vines.

This self-watering container stacks two 5-gallon plastic buckets on top of each other. A PVC spacer creates a reservoir for the excess water and acts as a wick to draw moisture into the roots of the plant.

Self-watering containers are commercially available or you can create your own from plans found online. One clever design incorporates an upright section of perforated PVC pipe in the center of the container, anchored with gravel and dirt before being surrounded by plants.

You can find many plans for these and other do-it-yourself watering systems online.

Rule № 3: Raise Your Sights

Whenever possible, plant in raised beds. Growing vining crops in raised beds is easier than growing ground-spreading plants because the beds need be only as wide as the base of the plants. Raised beds can be enclosed with a framework or simply mounded up and left freestanding. They can be as shallow as a few inches or as deep as a few feet, depending on your circumstances.

Design your raised beds to fit your physical ability and available space. The point is to work around them comfortably, without having to set foot in them.

The main advantage of piling up soil rich in organic matter is that the soil in the beds stays loose and friable. Why? Because there is more depth of organic matter/loose soil to begin with and because the beds are never stepped in. Raised beds provide better drainage, and the soil in raised beds warms more quickly in the spring than it does in a flat garden.

The easiest way to create raised beds is to plan your garden layout for the following spring during the fall and to set up the beds in advance. Fill and work in lots of organic matter (1 or 2 feet [61 cm] deep), and let the beds sit over the winter. (I use raw horse manure, as it has plenty of time to mellow.)

Rule № 4: Compost, Compost, Compost!

I can't repeat this enough. Organic matter, such as compost, straw, and rotted manure, degrades at warm temperatures (70°F [20°C] and above) to provide a constant, slow-release food for plant roots over the growing season.

It helps soil retain water and facilitates drainage by breaking up heavy native soils.

Soils rich in organic matter are less likely to compact. Compacted soils physically retard root growth and lack oxygen needed by plant roots. Degrading organic matter also generates small amounts of heat, helping to give you a head start on early planting seasons.

A lot of people don't like the idea of composting; they think it will be messy or smelly, but it's not if it's done properly. Composting is garden alchemy. Waste goes in; living gold comes out. And all your yard waste and kitchen scraps have to go someplace anyway, so why not into a tidy pile in a corner of the garden? If space is an issue, look online for plans for compact composters and worm farms made out of wood scraps, milk crates, plant pots, and other creative materials.

DON'T TOUCH: WET VINES

It's true that into every life a little rain must fall, but when it falls into the life of your garden, butt out. Rainfall, like the water from overhead sprinklers, has the unfortunate habit of landing on plant leaves and vines as much as it does on the ground.

This is nature's way and should be just fine, except that in nature, plants of the same species are not usually crammed together as closely as they are in our gardens.

Dripping and splashing water helps spread various pests and diseases, so avoid weeding, pruning, staking, and other garden tasks right after a shower.

TRAIN EARLY, TRAIN OFTEN

Just planting stakes next to your seedlings isn't enough. You still have to keep an eye on your support system. The key to getting your plants to grow up a support is physically guiding them on their way up. Make it a habit to check every few days to see if vines need to be placed on the next level of a support, twisted around a pole, or woven through netting to keep them on track. The growing tips are much more flexible than any other part of the vine and easiest to bend or move.

The earlier you train, the easier it is. Move vines only as far as they easily allow. If you need to make a major adjustment, do it over a period of days, a little at a time. It's a hands-on thing to learn. The more vines you handle, the more you'll get the feel of how easy they are to manipulate at which stage.

Rule № 5: A Stake in Time

Your tomato plants are flourishing, so you decide it's about time to start training them. But something comes up to keep you away from the garden. Several days later, you notice they are beginning to sprawl, so you go out and get busy.

Trouble is, you inadvertently break off a few vining stems as you work to control them, and perhaps you step on and crush one or two. But finally, you get all those vines collected and tied to a support, and as a last fail-safe measure, you pound a few stakes into the ground to anchor it. Weeks later, you notice some of the plants are flagging and realize that you drove the stakes right through the feeder roots.

Plant parenthood means supporting your plants from the get-go. Put in stakes, trellises, fences, and so on at the same time the plants go into the ground. It's also the best way to account for the mature size of the plant and not overcrowd your garden space with more plants than you have plot.

Rule № 6: Mulch Ado about Nothing

Mulching, the practice of covering up bare ground to slow water evaporation from the soil, is the last word in conserving water, and then some. A layer of mulch also shades roots, much appreciated by many types of plants, and prevents weed seeds from getting a roothold. An organic mulch, such as straw or partially decomposed compost, gives the added benefit of slowly feeding and amending the soil when it is tilled or dug in at the end of the season.

Some inorganic mulches, such as clear, red, or black plastics, can help to warm the soil and reflect the sun's rays. Mulching is a good all-around practice that saves water, work, and weeding and will benefit all of your garden crops.

Rule № 7: Weed 'em and Reap

No matter how much you mulch, it is inevitable that weeds will still find a way in. They may be wildflowers by another name, but weeds can provide a breeding ground for diseases and shelter hordes of insect pests. They steal water and nutrients directly from crop roots and, if allowed to grow, can shade them out of their fair share of sunlight.

Keep weeds at bay early and often by hand pulling or shallow cultivation with a hoe or other garden tool. Shallow cultivation, either under mulch or in its absence, has the advantage of disturbing the soil surface, which helps water absorption. Undisturbed soil

KEEP RECORDS

Someone asked me just this year how many pounds of food I expected to get out of my garden. I had no clue. Talk about a sin of omission.

I like to keep records of which varieties I plant, when they produce first fruits, when pests appear (deer usually don't bother until August, the bleeping ground squirrels have a heyday in May, and yellow jackets take over in late summer), temperatures, rainfall, and so on. It allows me the illusion that I am in control.

And keeping records of what is planted where, from season to season, is critical to effective crop rotation. Some crops shouldn't set root in the same spot for three or four years. Who remembers for that long?

settles and compacts into a crust that prevents water from penetrating down to plant roots.

Rule № 8: Round and Round We Go

Or in other words, rotate your crops. Planting different types of crops in different areas of your garden each season helps avoid a myriad of problems that can plague your plants if they are grown in the same spot season after season.

Soilborne pests and diseases multiply if provided with their favorite hosts year after year; simply planting a different crop interrupts the life cycle of plant-specific pests.

Rotating crops also helps to stabilize the nutrient balance of soils, as deep-rooted crops help pull up phosphorus and potassium from the soil depths and legumes restore nitrogen. By alternating heavy feeders such as brassicas (e.g., cabbages, turnips, kale), tomatoes, and corn with those that feed the soil, such as peas, beans, and cover crops, and never planting the same crop in the same spot two years in a row, you can greatly reduce the likelihood of certain plant diseases while helping to maintain soil fertility.

CHAPTER 2

MAKING
THE
MOST
OF MATERIALS

The building materials you choose for your vertical gardening structures depend on your answers to a few questions. How much can you spend on aesthetics? Are you building a temporary (single-season) structure or a permanent addition to the garden? What type of plants do you want to support? What's your style? Do you prefer a sleek, modern look or something more rustic?

Many gardeners (and I'm one of them) like to be creatively frugal by recycling items such as baling twine, 10-gallon pails, and leftover lumber. Always remember that one man's trash is another man's trellis. A scrap-lumber structure may not be as visually appealing as is a custom-made redwood grape arbor, but both serve the purpose equally well. Creative designing and lush, healthy foliage will soon obscure any less-than-attractive components.

BUILDING A FRAMEWORK

Most trellises have two basic parts, a frame and a support system, in a wide range of variations. The frame is usually constructed of stiff, sturdy, weight-bearing material, such as lumber, metal, or heavy bamboo. It is generally built of vertical standards with horizontal beams, wires, or slats running between them to give the frame shape. But of course there are exceptions (see chapter 3).

The frame also holds up the plant supports, the part of the trellis to which plants are directly affixed. Plant supports may be made from the same material as the frame but are often constructed of a lighter, more flexible material, such as twine, netting, or wire.

A sturdy wooden trellis or A-frame is versatile, can support a wide variety of crops, and can be used year after year if properly stored over the winter.

Workable Wood

Wood is by far the most common material used in building trellises and other frames. It is sturdy and attractive, and some types will last a lifetime. It is not the cheapest option, especially if you select high-quality wood, but the more expensive kinds of wood will repay you with years of low-maintenance service.

The best woods for garden use are cedar, redwood, black locust, cypress, spruce, Osage orange, and oak — any of these may last for decades. They are more weather resistant than cheaper pine or fir, which will rot in a few years if left untreated. Pressure-treated pine and fir will last much longer than untreated, but could be saturated with chemicals that you may not want to introduce into your garden (see Chemicals to Keep Away From, below).

No matter what type of wood you choose for a support system, look for posts cut from the center of the tree — the heartwood. Untreated heartwood posts last twice as long as untreated wood cut from the outside edges — the sapwood.

Another type of wood to use as building material is any green, flexible wood. Willow is the classic example, but any wood that is fresh enough and thin enough to bend can be used to fashion bentwood fences, trellises, and other garden structures.

> To extend the life of trellises constructed of wood, design them to knock down and store away when not in use, and store them out of winter weather.

CHEMICALS TO KEEP AWAY FROM

Wood treated with **creosote** is not recommended for garden use because it is toxic to plants. **Copper naphthenate** (heavy Cuprinol, Tenino Copper Naphthenate) is often recommended for use on wood for garden structures, but according to manufacturers' labels it is *not* suitable for food garden use.

Clear Cuprinol, also often recommended for use in food-garden construction, contains 3-iodo-2-propynyl butyl carbamate — designated by the Pesticide Action Network (PAN) as a Bad Actor chemical for acute toxicity.

You may save money by substituting scrap lumber for new, but take care in using any old wood that has been painted, as old paint may be lead based. The bottom line is either use high-quality wood to begin with or factor in the cost of replacing cheaper wood every few years. I don't recommend taking your chances with chemically treated wood.

Metal cages like this one are readily available for individual plants, but you can build a whole support system from metal pipe that will last for years and can be designed for any space.

Heavy Metal

Galvanized steel fence posts come in various lengths from 4 to 8 (1–2 m) long and are readily available from farm supply stores. Perhaps not as good-looking as wooden posts, they are sturdy, easy to install, easy to take out, last forever, and, most important, do the job.

> Some designs that use pipe incorporate an underground portion that is drilled with drainage holes to irrigate plants at root level.

Metal pipe, either salvaged or purchased new, is also good framing material. Galvanized pipe will outlast nongalvanized pipe, except in seaside areas, where damp, salty air speeds corrosion. The pipe can be driven into the soil and is easily removed if necessary. Fittings, such as Ts, Ys, and elbows, give the trellis designer many options. Short pieces can be connected; corners, arms, or extensions can be added; and entire sections can be fitted together or altered. A little elbow grease and a hacksaw are all you need to shorten long pieces.

FORGET DIY
Let the Pros Do It for You

Not everyone has the time, know-how, or inclination to build a garden's worth of support systems. Fortunately, a range of ready-made trellises and trellising materials can be found from a variety of sources.

★ **Precast metal trellis panels,** from frugally functional to divinely decorative, are available in any style imaginable.

★ **Circular or square tomato cages** fit over small plants and support them as the plants grow through the rings, and some can be stacked to accommodate vigorous vines.

★ **Pole bean and tomato towers** come complete with framework and supports up to 6 feet (2 m) tall.

★ **Obelisks, tuteurs, tripods,** and **lattice frames** can be works of art in their own right and wonderfully functional additions to your garden space.

Lightweight and practical, wire mesh products allow you to customize your trellis dimensions to your plot and crop. See Resources for suppliers of these and other useful items.

Practical Plastic

Pipe made from PVC (polyvinyl chloride) may win even more votes as a suitable framing material counterpart. PVC pipe comes in many sizes, shapes, and varieties, including rigid with thick walls or thin and flexible. Like metal pipe, different fittings make it easy to plan a multitude of useful garden designs, from full-scale arbors to individual plant cages. Whether you like the look of PVC is your decision, but it is very durable and reasonably priced.

The biggest concern with PVC is its environmental impact from start to finish. Although safe for garden use, it is manufactured of extremely toxic substances, and according to the Association of Post Consumer Plastics Recyclers, it is not feasibly recyclable.

Beautiful Bamboo

Bamboo is lightweight and weathers as well or better than scrap lumber. It tends to split, though, if you try to bend it, especially if it is cold. Compared to most other building materials, it is very inexpensive.

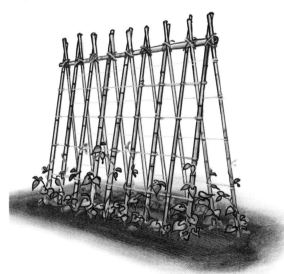

Bamboo is an inexpensive, durable, and useful material in the garden.

In some climates, bamboo can also be grown at home to provide you with lots of free building material. Just as attractive as wood, it can be used in many designs as both framing and support material.

DESIGNING YOUR SUPPORT SYSTEM

The type of plant support you use in your design, like the material used for framing, depends greatly on the type of plant it must support. Most garden crops can be trained up twine, netting wire, or wire mesh.

Wooden lattice, though more expensive, is often used for permanent landscaping trellises that are destined for the swarming vines of heavy crops like squash and melons and grapes. If you do buy lattice, make sure it's sturdy to begin with, or it'll just fall apart and cost more to replace.

Avoid flimsy string that will break under the weight of growing vines. Fine, taut string can slice through growing vines, cut off a plant's circulation, and kill the vine.

Twine, String, or Rope

Twine or heavy string is a garden trellis institution. Heavy-duty jute is a natural, compostable fiber and is almost universally available and fairly cheap. Nylon seine twine, cotton cable cord, and vinyl-coated clothesline wire are all reusable possibilities. Any old rope you have lying around, including nylon, plastic, jute, or braided or plaited anything, will do nicely for a plant support. Natural fibers, however, tend to swell and shrink as they get wet then dry and are susceptible to rot.

Baling twine is available for the asking, depending on where you live. Miles of it are cast out every day by livestock owners who would probably be happy to have you remove it for them. (You may even pick up some free fertilizer in the bargain!)

Check out stables, racetracks, dairies, hobby farms, petting zoos, or anyone who may feed animals hay; they are big users of bales held together by twine. Alfalfa is often put up in large bales and held with wire rather than twine; this wire is flexible, lightweight, and strong enough to weave into a trellis design.

As mentioned earlier, ready-made netting for garden trellises is sold through mail-order catalogs and garden supply stores (see Resources). It is woven of strong, weatherproof nylon with large 6- to 7-inch (15–18 cm) square openings to allow for easy pruning, tying, inspecting, and harvesting. Available in different widths and lengths, netting is moderately priced and will last many seasons.

Wire and Mesh

Wire can be substituted for twine or netting and is the first choice for some plants. Ten-gauge copper or galvanized wire, 3/16-inch vinyl-coated tiller cable, guy wire, baler wire, or salvaged electrical or telephone wire can be strung along your frames.

Use ready-made stock panels to create strong support systems for a variety of plants. The openings must be large enough to admit your hand for easy harvesting.

Wire-mesh fencing is a great choice to incorporate into a trellis. Galvanized, woven-wire mesh (also called sheep or hog wire) performs admirably, has a rustic look, will last for years, and is more rust resistant and more expensive than nongalvanized wire mesh, such as concrete reinforcing wire. Avoid chicken wire (also called poultry wire or netting). The wire is flimsy and the openings are too small to work with comfortably.

Rigid, heavy-duty "wire" stock panels (also called sheep panels, hog panels, or cattle panels) come standard in 16-foot (5 m) lengths and are very useful for fencing as well as for building trellises. The wire is actually a

THINKING AHEAD

It is very important to choose a wire with a large enough mesh (4- to 6-inch [10–15 cm] openings) to comfortably fit your hand through. Smaller wire mesh presents two frustrating problems. First, a tighter mesh may not allow the fruits of your labor to be easily tended or picked. No amount of swearing will put a 4-inch-wide squash through a 2-inch-square hole!

Second, pulling dead vines out of small wire mesh at the end of the season is a chore that no gardener should have to add to his or her list of fall cleanup duties.

THINKING OUTSIDE THE A-FRAME

You'd be amazed at what kinds of things plants will grow vertically on, as long as the supports are strong enough and there are plenty of footholds for those grabbing tendrils and curling vines. People have created support systems out of chain-link fences, sections of old porch railings, the mattress supports from cribs, ladders, wooden pallets, and more. Plants can be trained to grow over fire escapes, up walls, and along staircases to decks and balconies.

Once you start looking around for vertical space, you might be surprised to see just where vegetables can grow. I know someone who nailed lattice to one side of her kids' wooden play structure and grew beans up it. After the kids grew up, she replaced the swings with a hanging bench and turned the sandbox into a raised bed with climbing cucumbers in back and peppers in front.

welded grid of rigid, cast, galvanized rods, available in 6 gauge (0.194 inch thick), 4 gauge (0.225 inches thick) and 2¾ gauge (¼ inch thick). Panels average about 35 pounds (16 kg) each. Some places sell a 6-gauge utility panel that varies in height and is 20 feet (6 m) long with 4-inch (10 cm) openings, but these may be harder to find than standard stock panels.

> Always use galvanized nails or staples with galvanized wire and nongalvanized fasteners with nongalvanized fencing to prevent corrosion at contact points.

One drawback to wire or wire mesh is that it is not always suitable for quick-growing, tender annual vines. In some areas, the wire becomes very hot under the summer sun and can burn sensitive vines and foliage.

A quick fix is to wrap exposed metal parts with florist tape. Over time, growth will shade the metal and thereby minimize the risk of it burning foliage. But if your garden tends to

heat up quickly and metal gets untouchably hot, consider using another type of material to support tender plants.

Wood and Bamboo

Wood lathing or poles can be used for plant supports in designs from arbors and arches to tepee-style trellises. Trimmed saplings make excellent rustic poles and, if peeled and cured in the sun, will last for several seasons.

Bamboo rods used as plant supports give a rustic/exotic look and a durable future to any trellis. They are available online, in catalogs, and at some garden supply stores.

Ties, Clips, and Slings

Some plants climb by means of spiraling tendrils or leafstalks; some by stems that weave in and out of or wrap around available supports; and still others by aerial, rootlike holdfasts or tiny, adhesive pads that cling to their supporting surface. Any of these, at some point, may need a little assist to stay aloft.

A variety of ties, clips, slings, and other accessories can be used in training upwardly mobile vines. (See page 96 for more on slings).

For garden crops, usually all that is needed is to gently guide the stems to the support and watch them climb. Some, however, need to be tied in place as they grow.

Seed catalogs, gardening websites, and garden supply stores offer soft twist ties and clips especially made for securing delicate plant stems to trellises, stakes, fencing, or twine (see Resources). As with many gardening supplies, homemade substitutes abound — jute cord; plastic ties; paper-covered, wire twist ties; lengths of vinyl-covered wire or twine; plastic grocery bags; and strips of old cloth or discarded nylons can all be put to good use.

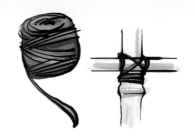

Commercial clips and ties are often handy and reusable, but a simple ball of twine has many uses in the garden.

> Tying vines too tight will constrict the vascular system of a plant and cut off the flow of nutrients. Slip knots may accidentally tighten, with the same results.

Other hardware that you may need in building your trellis or managing your vines can include nails and staples; turnbuckles, to keep weight-bearing wires taut; eyebolts and wire rope clips, to hold wires or twine; and hinges and floor flanges, or other fastening devices to secure wires in place.

Setting Up Slings

The fruit of some vines may require additional support as it grows. The weight of squash, pumpkins, and melons can pull on the trellised vines and cause them to sag or break. Why risk the unnecessary splattering

FIT TO BE TIED
Keeping Your Plants on the Up and Up

TIE TYPE	PROS	CONS
Commercial plant ties	Soft, pliable, reusable, can be cut to size, almost unseen in garden	Minor expense
Rag ties	Soft, pliable, usually reusable, can be cut to size, free	Can be unsightly
Salvaged twist ties	Free, easily maneuvered with one hand	Often not sturdy enough or too short
Plastic bags	Strong, durable, free, plentiful	Can be unsightly, hard to untie
Zip ties	Strong, easy to use	Not reusable, often too short, hard to remove

of a prize melon when a little prevention will stop the unthinkable?

You can buy ready-made fruit supports (designed to be put on while the fruit is small and then stretch as the fruit matures), but old panty hose, cut-up bed linens or T-shirts, bird netting, or any other handy fabric can be fashioned into a lifesaving sling.

1. Cut the material to the appropriate size for the fruit, judging by its predicted size and weight at maturity.

2. Tie one end securely to the plant support and loosely fit the fabric under the fruit; center it in the sling as much as possible.

3. Tie the other end of the sling to the plant support so that the fruit rests loosely and comfortably in its little hammock.

BEING CREATIVE WITH CONTAINERS

It is true that many gardeners turn to trellising crops because they're short on space and only then realize the other bonuses of vertical gardening. But if you are really squeezed for ground space, perhaps to where you don't own even a small backyard or garden plot, consider container gardening.

Almost anything that can be trellised can be reared in some type of planter box. Many plans for build-your-own planters incorporate a trellis right into the design. Or you can purchase containers, such as large clay or fiber pots, redwood boxes, and half wine barrels, and attach a trellis yourself. Be sure that the container has never contained any type of toxic substance. Drill holes in the bottom for adequate drainage and place the container in a sunny spot.

Potential mini-gardens are all around; you just have to think like a creative scavenger. Consider industrial shipping crates, including food-industry intermediate bulk containers (or IBCs for short), laundry tubs, livestock watering tanks, discarded bathtubs, plastic soap barrels from your local carwash, even recycled recycling containers!

CHAPTER 3

TRADITIONAL TECHNIQUES

{ TEPEES AND TRELLISES }

The design of your support systems depends on several things. You must consider the type of plants you want to grow (two or more types of vines can happily coexist on one structure), the materials that you have to work with, and the style of support system you want. Nature and finances may rule the first two considerations, but the style is limited only by your imagination and the laws of physics.

Picture an arch-framed garden gate overflowing with spectacular scarlet runner beans, first in full bloom and then producing piles of tasty beans. What could be lovelier? To the avid recycler, tomato towers built from old bicycle wheels or a pea trellis fashioned from a discarded mattress frame can be beautiful. In the garden, function is at least as important as form. To a gardener, any healthy vine winding up any type of trellis is a pretty sight.

STARTING WITH STAKES

The simplest of all plant supports are individual stakes or poles. Drive one into the soil near the base of a plant, and the vines instinctively latch on to them. Well, it's almost that easy.

Tomato stakes and bean poles are classic examples. At transplant time, or as a plant begins to show distinct vining growth (a few inches is enough to get it started in the right direction), gently tie the stem near the base of the stake. As the plant grows, continue to tie it at intervals along the stake to support the vine. Once the plant reaches the full height of the stake, prune excess growth that continues past the top.

Most garden centers offer a range of wooden, bamboo, and manufactured stakes that are suitable for training tomatoes, beans, squash, and other annual vines. Scrap lumber in 1×2 or 2×2 sizes, sturdy saplings, pipe, rebar, or another rigid material can also be commandeered for service.

TERRIFIC TEPEES

Why settle for one stake or pole, when a bunch of them will support more plants plus add a touch of imagination to your garden? There is a primitive beauty in greenery swirling its way up the legs of a tepee support. The ancient design conjures up images of gardeners of long ago. The form lends itself to many plants, from beans, peas, and tomatoes to heavy-fruited crops such as melons and squash. Many vines are light enough to be supported on sapling poles or bamboo, but those that bear heavy fruit require a sturdier structure. Building a tepee is quick, easy, and inexpensive.

A tepee of lightweight bamboo poles provides a traditional support system for beans and peas.

A Small Tepee

One person can set up a small tepee alone, but it sure makes the job go faster with a helper. You will need 4 to 12 poles — thin ones for flowers, peas, or beans, and stouter ones for squash, melons, or heavy sweet potato vines. Cut the poles to the desired length, adding 1 to 2 feet (30–61 cm) to the height of your finished structure. *Note*: You probably don't want your tepee to be taller than you are!

A tepee is a great way to get kids excited about growing food, because as the vines cover it, the tepee creates its own secret garden, complete with snacks!

If you ever thought algebra was a waste of time, here's one case where it comes in handy. Use the Pythagorean theorem $(a + b^2 = c^2)$ to calculate exact lengths of tepee poles by using c for the length of the pole, a for half the width of the overall tepee on the ground, and b for the total height of the structure.

1. Use twine, raffia, wire, or strips of cloth to lash the poles together, about a foot (30 cm) from the top. To do this, pull the poles into a tight bundle; wrap the twine around the bundle a few times, weaving in and out of the poles as well as looping around them; and then tie it snugly.

2. Prop the bundle of poles over the prepared soil and position the bottom ends equal distances apart in a circle. It works best to just prop the thing up in whatever form it will stand on its own, then work your way around it, positioning each leg to a point on a circle.

3. Push the end of each pole into the soft earth to help stabilize the tepee until growing plants can anchor it in place. Each leg should be able to support one to three vines. If high winds, cats, or other forces of nature threaten to topple your tepee, drive stakes at regular intervals around the base and lash each (or every other) leg to a stake. Or try anchoring your poles with cinder blocks or in buckets of sand.

A Large Tepee

Larger poles, 2 to 3 inches (5–8 cm) across, are heavy enough to be freestanding. There is usually no need to drive them into the soil or to stake them. Their extra weight makes it nearly impossible to erect the tepee all at once as described above, and you'll need a helper. The tried-and-true method for erecting a large tepee is to first set up a tripod, then add as many extra legs to the structure as you desire. In addition to the poles, you'll need about 20 feet (6 m) of twine or light rope.

It's important to choose stakes that are as long as your plant will be tall at maturity.

1. To build your tepee, lay out three poles near where the finished structure will stand. Position them so that two are together and the third is off to one side; together they should form a V.

2. Tie the twine or rope around and between the ends of the three poles, about 1 foot (30 cm) from the top, to secure them together. Leave several feet of rope loose so you can attach the remaining poles.

Heavy poles set firmly in the ground can take the weight of several squash or bean vines.

3. Stand back at the end of the rope and pull to raise the tepee to its feet. While you hold the rope, have your helper move one of the two poles that were together to an independent third position.

If you don't have a helper, use the rope to pull the three poles up to a point where their weight and the tension of the rope counterbalance to keep the poles in an almost upright position. Tie the rope to a fence, tree, truck bumper, or other fixed point to keep the tension, then position the feet of the poles where you want them.

4. With the tripod erected, the next step is to put up the rest of the poles. Place them so the feet are equidistant apart in a circle

MALABAR SPINACH: TRY SOMETHING NEW

For something unusual in the greens department, try Malabar spinach (*Basella alba*). Native to the tropics of Africa and southern Asia, this edible vine makes a wonderful summer spinach substitute; though it needs a lot of water, it flourishes in the hot weather that makes a regular spinach wilt or bolt.

This handsome plant may well become the centerpiece of your garden; it is as distinctively attractive as it is manically productive. Trained to a support, the majestic size of the plant, with vines from 20 to 30 feet (6–9 m) long, commands attention. The dark green, heart-shaped, fleshy leaves and bright red or contrasting white stems have a mild flavor.

Planting Guidelines

Malabar spinach loves to soak up the sun, but will also grow in partial shade. Owing to its native habitat, it tolerates poor soils, but a healthy dose of compost or rotted manure worked in at transplant time will give a nutrient boost to get this green giant off to a jolly good start.

As a fleshy-leafed plant, it requires plenty of water. It grows as a perennial in Zones 10 and 11, but if you live in an area with frost, consider it an annual.

Training Malabar Spinach to Grow Up

This plant is almost too easy to grow! Malabar spinach is a vigorous, climbing vine that twines its stem around a support. Twine, wire, poles, and fence-type frames are all suitable, but whatever you use must be sturdy enough to support the weight of the vines.

The trailing stems may need a little initial guidance in finding their support. If you gently lean them against the lower levels of the trellis in the beginning, they should grow in the right direction.

Enjoying Your Harvest

Plants can endure a little harvesting as soon as there are several sets of full-sized leaves, or once stem tips reach 6 to 8 inches (10–15 cm) in length (55–70 days after seeding). Both stems and leaves can be harvested throughout the season, resulting in thicker, lusher, very tender new growth. Thin regularly, as leaves and stems become tough as they mature.

Both shoots and leaves can be served either fresh or as cooked greens. The leaves are mucilaginous, which makes them great for thickening soups, but they are easily overcooked. A staple of many Asian cultures, they fit right into lots of Asian recipes, including stir-fries.

They are a natural for salads, in sandwiches, or in any recipe you would normally use spinach. Great in omelets, they tend to thicken quiches, so use them according to your preference. Use fresh leaves right away, as they tend to get slimy after a few days.

A running tepee

and they intersect at about the same spot at the top. The weight of each pole against the others stabilizes the tepee.

5. Finally, take the end of the rope and walk around the tepee a few times, looping the rope up and around the tops of the poles where they intersect to lash them together. This forms a large, solid, heavy-duty structure that can serve as a temporary or semi-permanent plant support for any plant that trails or vines.

A Four-Legged Tepee

Here's a quick cheater method for a smaller, lighter, four-legged tepee: Bundle two pairs of poles, lashing them together about a foot (30 cm) from one end. Raise one pair of poles into position, then have a helper hold the poles in place while you straddle them with the second pair. Arrange the legs, then wrap the tops together. A four-legged tepee (two sets of two poles) works wonderfully for squash, melons, and sweet potatoes.

The Running Tepee

Another variation on the tepee method is a running tepee. Running tepees are great for long, wide rows of crops. Seed directly or transplant along the length of each row that is created by the feet of the tepee poles.

To build one, you need a collection of poles (saplings, scrap 1×2s, and bamboo are perfect), plus six larger ones or a couple of solid posts to anchor them and sturdy twine to tie the whole thing together.

1. Start with either a three-pole tepee or a post at each end of the row; a height of 6 feet will accommodate most crops.

2. Tie a long, thin pole to the top of the end tepees or posts so that it connects the two, or string a heavy wire or rope between the tops of the posts and tighten.

3. Lean the poles along the length of the connecting pole in pairs and tie each pair together at the top.

YOU SAY TEPEE, I SAY TUTEUR

Additional support for heavy vines can be worked into a tepee design by wrapping heavy twine or rope around the legs, starting about 1 foot (30 cm) from the bottom and working up and around toward the top. Technically, a tepee with horizontal rungs (whether they be rope, willow twigs, or copper tubing) is called a *tuteur* (French for "to train" or "to guide").

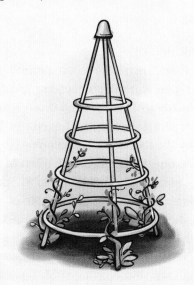

Some are quite decorative and can add a fanciful aura to a functional piece of garden hardware. By placing containers at various heights inside a sturdily built tuteur, you can further increase the growing space and plant a variety of plants in one spot.

Let them intermingle, or prune them so that some climb to a height of about 4 feet, while others start at that height (the height at which their container rests inside the tuteur) and continue up.

SELF-CONTAINED TRELLISING

Planting vining crops in containers can dramatically reduce your need for ground space — you don't even need a yard! Just remember that containers need special growing mediums and regular watering (sometimes more than once a day in hot/dry weather).

Another consideration for containers is that they be large enough to accommodate the roots of any given plant or plants. A half wine barrel, for instance, will hold several healthy bean or pea plants, two or three cucumbers or melons, one or two squash or pumpkin plants, or about ten trailing strawberries.

Using containers with trellises or tepees adds countless ways of incorporating lots of plants together; you can create a living wall of vegetation that serves as both a sound/privacy screen and gardener's buffet. Build some shelves to rest the containers on, or hang them on a trellis or wall. Just be sure the structure is sturdy enough to support the combined weight of containers, soil mix, and water, not to mention the plants themselves.

Using containers with trellises gives you all kinds of options for maximizing space in your garden.

A fence trellis

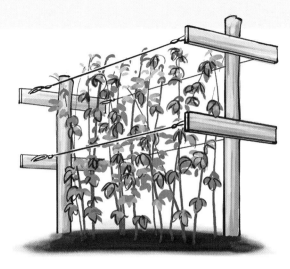

A clothesline trellis

FENCES MAKE FINE TRELLISES

Fences are among the easiest, most versatile, and most commonly used trellises found in gardens everywhere. If you don't have an actual fence to grow against, drive a post at each end of a garden row and place other posts in between as needed for support. String with twine, wire, netting, or wire mesh, and you have a fence-type trellis. The standards, or end posts, can be anything from wood or metal fence posts to metal or PVC pipe. Tie, wire, staple, or nail the plant support to the standards so that it is taut enough to hold the vines without sagging.

Many trellises — from stake-and-netting dwarf pea fences to freestanding post-and-wire espalier trellises — follow this simple design. Some need bracing at the end posts or additional posts in between, depending on the length of the fence and the amount of weight they must support.

One design trick that makes harvesting easier is to rig a fence-type trellis at an angle. The simplest way to do this is with premade wire panels, such as those used to create livestock fencing. Setting them up at an angle enables fruit to hang down freely between the spaces on the downhill side.

Rather than try to set support posts at an angle, set a post at each end of the panel, and one at the center if needed, and prop up the panel at an angle. You can fashion angle arms for added support, but generally the panels are stiff enough to stay put. (See illustration on page 84.)

Clothesline Trellis

By attaching crossarms to the end posts and running two (or more) wires between them, the simple fence trellis is converted into a clothesline trellis that can support multiple horizontal lines (usually made of wire) instead of just one.

This type of trellis allows you to plant double rows and is useful for berry patches and for many annual crops such as peas and beans. Because the posts in clothesline trellises must bear more weight than those in a simple fence, it is a good idea to brace them at each end.

To erect a clothesline trellis, you'll need posts for uprights; pipes, lumber, or poles for crossarms and braces; wire; eyebolts; and tensioners. Whether you use wood or steel posts is just as much a matter of preference as it is of convenience and cost. Steel posts are easily pounded into the ground, while wooden posts are generally set the old-fashioned way — by digging a hole 2 feet [61 cm] deep and tamping the earth back into it as the post is held steady. Some folks will even secure a post with cement in the hole, obviously something reserved for permanent structures.

Metal fence posts can be removed from soft garden soil almost as easily as they can be pounded in, making them the best choice for single-season standards. If you are using wood, construct the entire post setup before pounding it into the ground. A 3- to 4-foot (1 m) crossbeam on an 8-foot (2.4 m) post, complete with 2-foot-long (61 cm) braces, will hold just about any trailing vine (or a few loads of clothes!).

Connect the wire either by looping it around the crossarms or by wrapping it around eyebolts set into the crossarms for that purpose. Wire can be tightened by hand or pulled taut with tensioners.

If the lines start to sag, check to be sure the posts are not being pulled toward one another. If they are, a quick fix is to prop them up with braces that run from the top or middle of the post down to the ground. Either toe-nail these braces into the post or wedge them in place securely.

COOL CAGES

Another simple and efficient method of containing an errant sprawler is with a cage. Cages can be nailed together from scrap 1×2 lumber or made with wire mesh. Choose a wire mesh that is sturdy enough to retain its shape under the weight of vines and fruit and has openings big enough for you to reach through when harvesting. Bend the mesh into a cylinder or an arch shape and arrange it around or over young transplants.

Round or square cages, 2 to 3 feet (61–91 cm) in diameter and 3 to 4 feet (91–121 cm) high, will both contain and support a variety of vines. You can calculate exact measurements using the old standby $C = 2(pi)r$ or simply estimate a 6½-foot length of wire mesh for a 2-foot-diameter cage, 20 feet for a 3-foot-diameter cage, or 25 feet for a 4-foot-diameter cage. Wire mesh comes in varying heights and 50-foot lengths or longer, so one roll can make at least two cages, depending on their diameters.

1. Connect snaps to the ends of the mesh and snap the cylinders together, or instead, when cutting the wire, add a few inches to the finished measurement.

2. Wrap the wire into a cylinder and bend the cut ends of the wire back over the opposite end of the mesh to hold it in place.

SPIRALING INTO CONTROL

A fun, whimsical, and surprisingly practical variation is a spiraling metal stake. I've found them in 3½-foot and 7-foot (1–2 m) lengths, but other sizes are bound to be available.

The idea is that the spiral shape offers just enough of a horizontal surface to allow plants to grab on and continue up the vertical portions of the stake. Clever and cute, but I'm still trying to figure out ways to build my own!

Building your own wooden tomato cages takes an investment of time and materials, but if built well, they'll last for years and can be used to train up other veggies as well.

3. Drive a stake or two into the ground through the wire mesh to anchor the support against the wind.

More intricate designs can be constructed by using lighter-weight wire attached to wooden frames or by cutting the wire mesh into individual panels and wiring them together into freestanding square cages. The advantage of panel-type cages is that they can be taken apart for storage. For a square or panel-type cage, multiply the width of the cage by 4 and cut the wire accordingly, adding a few inches to overlap and connect the ends.

EXCELLENT A~FRAMES

The A-frame is an extremely useful, versatile, and easily constructed garden trellis. By incorporating either hinges or pivot nails into the top of an A-frame trellis, it can be folded together. This little bit of extra work during the design phase makes the structure a snap to move and store.

Another advantage to the A-frame design is that both sides of the trellis are used, creating a shaded corridor that is a perfect spot to plant some greens, which makes the row more productive.

An A-frame can be made sturdy enough to support even heavy crops, such as gourds and pumpkins. By changing its position in the garden every year, the same structure can support cucumbers one year, squash the next, then tomatoes, and later beans or peas.

It can also pull double duty by providing a framework for shade cloth and bug- or bird-proof crop covers or be turned into an instant greenhouse by tacking clear plastic sheeting to the frame. If versatility is not blessing enough from this useful design, consider that it can be built of scraps, which adds economy to the list of advantages.

Construct the A-frame of lightweight lumber: 1×2s or 2×4s. Wire-mesh fencing, garden

A series of wire mesh panels set in a zigzag pattern makes for easier picking come harvesttime.

netting, and vertically or horizontally strung wire or twine all serve well as the plant support. While you may design an A-frame in any dimensions to suit your site, bear in mind that if it is to be portable, it must be of manageable size. Better to build and move four 6-foot components than one 24-foot-long monster.

1. Cut lightweight stock panels in 6- to 8-foot (2–2.5 m) lengths with a bolt cutter.

2. Use a straightedge, such as a board or pipe, to bend the panels in the middle to form a V.

3. Flip the panels over, then place several of them along the row so that the ends are a few inches (about 8 cm) apart. The bends create an uninterrupted zigzag trellis.

4. Set the transplants in the spaces between the individual cages and train the vines up the sides of the cage on either side.

If you have the space, a quick and easy alternative is to lean two 16-foot (5 m) panels up against each other and wire them together at the top and/or put in posts at either end if you need added stability: that's it. Plant, water, weed, and harvest!

ARCHES AND ARBORS

Whether envisioning lush grapes, exotic wisteria, or romantic old country roses, most of us, when we dally on such thoughts, picture them clambering over some classic old arbor. Garden books, magazines, and websites are fairly bursting with patterns for beautiful, permanent landscape trellises. Often these structures serve as the focal point of the garden and set either a formal, informal, or rustic tone. We may not think of them as supports

An archway or arbor can support annual vines just as easily as it does more traditional roses or flowering vines.

for the vegetable garden, but a sturdily built permanent arbor is a perfect support for heavy crops — bountiful beans, melons, cucumbers, and even trailing squash or indeterminate tomatoes.

Architectural designs include rustic, prim Victorian, and sleek contemporary. You might lash large branches together for a rustic look or create swooping scrolls and archways for a formal approach. You can attach an arched trellis to a bare wall to convert it instantly into an elegant backdrop. Consider, however, attaching your elegant trellis with hinges or pivot bolts so that it can swing down if you ever need access to that wall.

The horizontal beams of an arbor provide not only a support for vines, but also a secluded, shady spot for the gardener. Doorways, paths, patios, gazebos, and any other special outdoor area can be transformed with a vine-covered archway. Consider including

A HYBRID SYSTEM

Something to try when planting lots of vining plants in a bed together is a cross between a cage and fence. A cagence? I've used this only with tomatoes, but the results were outstanding. It is quick and simple to install, virtually free (if you already have the fence posts and use leftover twine), not all that bad to look at, and easy to take down at the end of the season.

My growing beds are about 30 inches (76 cm) wide, so I pounded in a steel fence post at each corner of a 12-foot-long (3.6 m) bed and one at opposite sides in the middle. As the tomato plants grew, I wound twine (saved from hay bales) around the posts in a diamond pattern. Don't ask me the method of winding, I just kept going until I had the pattern I wanted.

As the tomatoes grow, they began to flop over their individual twine cages, so I put up another round of twine, about 8 inches (20 cm) higher than the first one. By the end of the season, I had five or six rounds of twine running up the posts for a total height of about 4 feet (1.2 m) and some very happy tomatoes.

a planter box in your designs, and enjoy the added benefits of raised beds.

Create a private corner with an arch or arbor, or use it as camouflage to hide trash cans or yard equipment. Living screens are also an excellent means of providing a windbreak or, to the often overwhelmed city dweller, a much needed noise and/or pollution barrier.

Practical Considerations

Despite the almost limitless possibilities for arbor design and construction, the gardener must always weigh the basic considerations of expense and the intended climbers. Posts should be driven or dug 24 to 30 inches (61–76 cm) deep or set in at least 18 inches (46 cm) of concrete.

The vertical supports should be well anchored with galvanized nails or screws to the horizontal beams that define the frame of the trellis. Horizontal supports must be strong enough to bear the weight of the vines; a double layer of crisscross lattice is sturdy and attractive.

Ease of maintenance should also be considered, not only for pruning, maintenance, and harvesting, but also for upkeep on the trellis and on any existing background structures. Brackets, bolts, hinges, and other hardware add somewhat to the initial investment but will go a long way toward making routine gardening chores easier by making the trellis — or at least parts of it — movable.

CHAPTER 4

NOT-SO-
TRADITIONAL
TRICKS

{ **HANGING, STACKING, TOWERING, AND MORE** }

Creative gardeners with limited space are always experimenting with ways to grow food up, and some of their solutions are nothing short of inspiring. If necessity is the mother of invention, a hunger for healthy homegrown food is its fairy godmother. Though trellising remains the most common method of vertical crop production, there are lots of other options for growing food in places you never thought possible. Even without a backyard to dig up, you can create your own small farm using containers in creative ways.

BEFORE YOU JUMP IN

The first rule for potted crops is to choose the right plants for the spot you have or the best spot (if you have more than one option) for the plants you want. This is just as critical to window or other container gardening as it is in any garden setting. In addition to the all-important sun, there are some other issues to consider.

Supply Sun and Shade

Be aware of how much sunlight your crop prefers. Most vegetables and herbs, but not all, adore full sun. Don't forget that full sun radiated by asphalt or reflected by a bright stucco wall is hotter and brighter than full sun in a deep green garden plot. Luckily, in the close quarters of a window box, some plants provide shade for their sun-sensitive neighbors. A south- or east-facing window,

CONTAINER PLANTING RECOMMENDATIONS

PLANT	MINIMUM SOIL DEPTH	MATURE SPACING	SUN/SHADE
Beans	6"	3–4"*	full sun
Beets	6"	2–3"	full sun
Broccoli	10"	12–18"	full sun
Carrots	8"	1–2"	full sun
Cucumbers	10"	6"	full sun
Eggplant	10"	10"	full sun
Flowers	6"	4–6"	full sun
Garlic	8"	2"	full sun
Herbs	6–8"	varies	full sun
Kale	8"	8"	sun to part shade
Lettuces	6"	4–6"	partial shade
Onions	8"	2–3"	sun to part shade
Peppers	8"	8–12"	sun
Radishes	4"	1–2"	sun to part shade
Spinach	4"	4–6"	partial shade
Summer squash	10"	2–3'	sun
Swiss chard	8"	6"	partial shade
Tomatoes (standard)*	12"	6–8"*	sun
Tomatoes (patio type)*	6–8"	4–6"*	sun
Winter squash*	10"	2–3'*	sun

Train vines up or let them dangle down the sides of the box. Larger fruit may need some support.

or something in between, usually produces the happiest plants.

Planters shaded by a building or wall to the south will not get enough sun to foster normal, healthy plant growth, and west-facing windows, especially on an apartment building, can toast plants to death. (If you have no choice other than a west-facing wall, try to arrange it so that you can shade plants during the most intense heat of the afternoon.)

Make Room for Roots

Use a container large enough to accommodate the roots of the crop you want to grow. For instance, tomatoes are deep rooted and need a pot or box at least 12 inches (30 cm) deep, whereas lettuce, bush beans, and beets will thrive in just 6 inches (15 cm). Container-grown plants are generally grown more closely together than their garden-ranging brethren, but you still have to consider the mature size of the plants you are growing and space them apart accordingly. (See the chart on page 32.)

Don't forget that because a tomato variety is small-*fruited*, it doesn't necessarily mean that the *plant* is small. Cherry tomato plants, for example, can grow to extreme lengths, so be aware of the growth habit of the variety you choose. Patio types are bred to be more compact, with less extensive root systems.

Deal with Drainage

Your watering system is a vital consideration. Planters dry out quickly, and those in full sun may need watering twice a day, but be cautious not to overwater. If drainage is inadequate, soggy roots will soon become sickly roots. A layer of gravel or broken pottery at the bottom of a container enables excess water to drain away.

WONDERFUL WINDOW BOXES

Window boxes are an old standby for those with limited growing space. One great thing about them is that you can tend to them from either outside or inside, depending on your living situation. A row of window boxes can line the railing of a deck or a single one can perch outside an apartment window several stories high. Combined with modern growing methods and materials, they can be more productive, with less work and in less space, than ever before.

You can insert a moisture meter to let you know exactly when to water, incorporate water-retaining hydrogels (high-tech gel particles that release water as the planting medium dries) into the soil at planting time, set up a window box to be self-watering, or even grow your veggies hydroponically (using all water and nutrients, no soil).

A simple window box can provide a quick and bountiful harvest of radishes, fresh tender greens, or herbs, or provide a crop of small-fruited trailing plants, such as grape and patio tomatoes.

Building Materials

Pine is the cheapest wood you can use, but it has to be primed and painted, or stained and sealed, which tends to offset the savings. A high-quality alkyd primer coat before painting prevents chemicals in the paint from leaching through the wood into the soil. A polyurethane sealant coat applied over stain will help preserve the wood and the color.

The best woods to use for building outdoor planters are cedar and redwood. They will outlast most other woods two or three times

A window box can provide space for a small climbing vegetable garden conveniently positioned just outside a kitchen window or on an apartment balcony.

over, naturally repel some pests, and need no coatings before use. You can paint or stain cedar or redwood if you like, but it's easier to allow these woods to weather naturally.

Fill 'er Up

One tip to extend window-box life is to not put soil directly into it. Build or buy a planter large enough that you can use plastic containers for the individual plants. The easiest thing is to use gallon-size nursery planters or water or milk jugs with the tops cut off. This practice helps to forestall the problems associated with inevitable wood rot because the wood stays much drier than if it was constantly in contact with wet soil. A bonus of the removable-container method is that you can replace sections of the window-box planting if needed (for harvesting, if a plant dies, or if you just want a change).

A HAPPY MEDIUM

When growing in pots, use a sterile (seed-free) growing medium, which will retain water well but won't compact as quickly or as much as plain dirt. A standard mixture is 1 part vermiculite or perlite to 1 part peat moss to 1 part compost or well-rotted manure with a handful or two of good garden soil (there *is* good stuff in real dirt) thrown in for good measure.

You can regulate the nutrient density of the soil by either adding finished compost every so often or feeding the soil with a commercial plant fertilizer. Soil pH and nutrient tests and meters — to ensure you get just the right amount of goodies to your plants' roots — are available for less than $20.

Keep It Fresh

Just how long your soil will last is another story. Even the best soil in containers compacts over time as its structure breaks down, affecting its ability to hold air. Without air, it can't provide optimal aeration and drainage to plant roots. Unfortunately, as critical as it is, aeration can't be adjusted during the growing season the way moisture or nutrient density can be.

Generally, by the end of the first season, 20 to 30 percent of the air capacity in a container is lost as the soil particles become smaller and therefore more tightly compacted. As much or more is lost the second year if the same soil is used again, as is, in the same container, and soil structure can be collapsed completely by the third year.

Gasping for Air

Plants "breathe" oxygen through their roots, but as the air-holding capacity of the planting medium declines, water retention goes up to the point that plant roots drown for lack of gas exchange. In addition, waterlogged soils tend to be acidic, harbor salts, and prevent plants from utilizing iron and other soil nutrients. The result is weak, yellow, dying plants.

The solution is simple — replace soil in containers annually (or at least amend it heavily with fresh soil mix). Using new soil also helps head off any soilborne pests, diseases, or fungi. Depleted soil can go into a compost heap or be mixed in with the regular garden soil, where it will continue to break down.

WINDOW FARMING

A very different sort of window gardening that is picking up momentum combines recycling old bottles, growing luscious edible plants, filtering summer sunlight (thus reducing cooling bills), and engaging fellow gardeners from around the world. It's called the **Windowfarms Project**.

Described as "a vitamin-rich living harvest and a lush trickling fountain-like curtain," window farming is a soilless way to grow food indoors. Plastic bottles are strung with tubing that provides water and nutrients, then hung in columns on the inside of a window to capture the sunlight and convert it into as many as 25 yummy, tender, nutritious plants at a time.

Based in New York, the Windowfarms Project encourages membership and innovative design based on the ideas presented on its website, *www.windowfarms.org.* Designs are free to members, with the condition that all information is shared freely among them. Preassembled grow kits are also available for purchase.

There are four kits, from the basic two-column Core Kit, containing eight hydroponic net cups, water-tube assemblies, filters, and more; to the deluxe, four-column Gourmet Kit, which includes hydroponic growing cups, bottles, and tubes, plus a state-of-the art quad-outlet electronic air pump, electric timer, and organic salad seeds.

Among other very doable options in vertical hydroponic gardening are PVC pipe systems and plastic barrel designs. **Easiest Garden** (*www.easiestgarden.com*) markets original plans and accessories. Its Vertical Garden has a footprint of less than 1 foot by 4 feet (30×121 cm). The design is ideal for strawberries, greens, and herbs.

Each system has four vertical pipes, each with nine preformed planting wells filled with an inert growing medium. Water sprays into the top of the pipes via a small fountain pump, flows through the roots into a reservoir, then recirculates to the top of the pipes. Videos on the website give step-by-step instructions.

It also offers plans for a Barrel Garden, from which you can build a space-intensive planting tower for pennies per planting pocket. The plans give information on converting various barrels — from 5-gallon (23 L) buckets up to 300-gallon (1,363 L) tanks — into gardens. On average, a standard 55-gallon (250 L) drum can foster 72 plants in pockets along the vertical face, with another dozen or so in the open top. That's a lot of green in very little ground space.

Don't forget that those plastic containers need to provide adequate water drainage. One solution is to place stones or pot shards in the bottom of the plastic planters. Another is to build the bottom of a window box out of hardware cloth, place your containers — with drainage holes in the bottom — in the mesh-bottomed box, and water at will.

Thinking Outside the Box

Of course, many types of vines will overflow the box and dangle merrily over the edge, but what about climbing vines? One way to incorporate them into a window box is to rig netting from the top of the window; one savvy design calls for rigging a sturdy curtain rod to the *outside* of the window. Training the vines is easy — just reach through either side of the window and weave them through or tie them to the netting as needed.

Another idea is to construct a window box about 2 feet (61 cm) wider than the window and attach a trellis to either side of the window (like shutters) on which to accommodate a climbing vine or two. One clever design has the trellises attached with hinges to 2×4s bolted to the window frame. The gardener can gently pull the trellises partially closed and safely harvest from indoors without having to lean out the window.

Don't use regular garden soil in containers, as it tends to compact and hinder root growth and water absorption.

Other ways to use a planter box to grow food up are designing it to fit over a deck railing, placing it on a shelving unit (ready-made stainless-steel hardware shelving racks won't rust, look attractive, and have their weight-bearing capacity printed right on the label), and custom building one to fit into an otherwise wasted corner or wall.

A window box can be bountiful as well as beautiful. Train a couple of cucumbers, cherry tomatoes, or pea vines to grow over a planting of greens or herbs.

JUST BAG IT!

An unusual option for hanging containers is to pop your plants into bags and hang them on hooks wherever is convenient. You can buy ready-made systems, but a little creative repurposing saves money and does good things for the environment. Here are some ideas for putting your garden in the bag.

Once you start looking at objects with an eye toward filling them with dirt and dropping in a plant or two, you'll be amazed at how your garden grows!

Sturdy canvas shopping totes hold a couple of gallons (9 L) of potting mix, and you can hang them wherever you've got some sunny vertical space.

A cloth shoe bag takes up little room while producing a variety of greens and herbs.

An old pair of jeans or shorts can be pressed into service with some sturdy sewing and a plastic liner.

Stacking a couple of hanging baskets over each other doubles your available vertical space on a porch or balcony.

GOOD OLD POTS AND PLANTERS

The trick to container gardening is to get the most growing space with the smallest footprint. One way to do this is to stack planters. Not surprisingly, several different brands of prefab, plastic, stackable planting pots are on the market, but you can get the same results with a little creative repurposing. Here are a few ideas to get you started (detailed plans for these designs and many variations on them are readily available online; see Resources).

Hang 'em High

One of the nicest things about a hanging basket is that you can fit in one or two just about anywhere. They add a touch of elegance and lushness to their surroundings, not to mention providing a convenient way to snag a snack. Other advantages are that the baskets can be lowered for watering, maintenance, and harvest, and they can be brought inside should frost, excessive heat, or high winds threaten.

One of the few disadvantages is that loose, dangling vines are particularly susceptible to battering, bruising, and breakage in high wind, so position them in sheltered spots. Hanging baskets need frequent watering, too.

HOW HEAVY IS DIRT?

Hanging plants must have a sturdy system to keep them in the air. Figuring the exact weight of a filled, growing planter is next to impossible, as the weight fluctuates with moisture content and the stage and success of the crop (lots of big, juicy, ripening tomatoes get heavy!), so it's best to calculate high. You don't want your baskets crashing down right after a thorough watering or after your carefully tended crops begin to ripen.

Although native soils weigh in at 100 pounds or more per cubic foot or roughly more than 13 pounds per gallon (7.48 gallons to the cubic foot), recommended planting mixes are much lighter.

★ Perlite: 5 to 8 pounds per cubic foot (up to a pound per gallon)

★ Dry peat moss: 30 to 40 pounds per cubic foot (4 or 5 pounds per gallon)

★ Compost: up to 150 pounds per cubic foot (20 pounds per gallon)

A mix of the three might weigh around 60 pounds a cubic foot (8 pounds per gallon). Factor in water weight, including the fact that peat moss can absorb 20 times its own weight in water.

Lots of nurseries are catching on these days and offering more than just petunias and fuchsias in preplanted hanging baskets. Tomatoes and strawberries are almost standard fare, but it's easy to create a custom hanging garden with just the plants you want.

Though many attractive styles of hanging pots and baskets are available — made of cheap vacuum-molded plastic, expensive molded plastic, pressed peat, and open wire, among other materials — what you can plant in them depends more on size than anything else. (See the chart on page 32 for recommended soil depths for planting.)

When planting cucumbers or squash, be especially careful, as they are fussy about transplanting and can sulk for weeks if their roots are overly disturbed.

You can make a particularly serviceable basket from a 5-gallon (23 L) plastic bucket (metal can transfer too much heat to the roots when hung in direct sunlight). New buckets or reclaimed former food containers are best; you'll know they have never contained any toxic substance. These buckets are large enough for deep-rooted container plants and sturdy enough to support a hefty crop. Fill the bottom 6 inches (15 cm) with pot shards or gravel to allow for drainage, or drill a dozen or so holes in the bottom to enable excess water to drain out.

Good-quality baskets, scrubbed and stored out of the weather for the winter, should last you several years. In the spring, give them a quick scrub, fill them with fresh growing medium, and you're good to go.

A popular option for tomatoes is the upside-down planter, easily fashioned from a 5-gallon bucket. The tomato grows out the bottom, leaving room at the top of the container for small root crops, herbs, or microgreens.

Upside-Down Danglers

There is definitely more than one way to hang a tomato plant. A popular trend in hanging baskets is the upside-down growing system, promoted primarily for tomatoes and strawberries, but doable for other plants that naturally trail, such as cucumbers, beans, and peas. Peppers and eggplant have also done acceptably well with this method.

Plants instinctively grow upward, and some interesting shapes will occur as they do.

Sometimes it helps to gently tie vines or stems in the desired direction or to brace or weight them as necessary to encourage the stems to grow out past the bottom of the container before branching upward. Otherwise, some try to grow into the bottom of the planter.

Various systems are sold ready-made, but you can make your own from a large plastic or peat pot or a 5-gallon (23 L) bucket. Here's how:

1. Install hanging hooks before you plant, making sure that they will bear the weight of the pot plus soil (don't forget that the soil will be wet!).

2. Cut or drill a hole in the bottom of a planter for each plant. For large plants such as tomatoes, one hole per container, dead center, 1 or 2 inches (2.5–5 cm) in diameter, works well. For smaller plants, such as pole beans and peas, use six to eight holes maximum, and for peppers, eggplant, and strawberries, three or four is sufficient. Holes need to be large enough to fit transplants through, either head (foliage) first or feet (roots) first, as well as large enough to accommodate the stem of the plant once it matures.

3. Hang the bucket and thread each plant through a hole either by carefully pushing the root-ball from the outside of the planter in or by very gently pulling the leaves through from the inside.

4. Once the seedling is in place, add moistened planting soil, a little at a time, gently pressing it as you go, until the transplant is stable. If you're putting in more than one plant, add some potting medium around each one to help hold it in place as you put in the others.

5. Continue adding soil to within 2 to 4 inches (5–10 cm) of the top. Water until the excess starts to drain out the bottom.

The art of growing upside-down plants is as much about experimentation and having fun with interesting plants as it is about harvest. The upside is that you'll never have to pull a weed. The open top end of the bucket can be mulched or put to work growing micro greens, small root crops (radishes, baby carrots, small beets), and herbs, or even trailing nasturtiums and other edible flowers to add visual appeal.

> Make sure your support system is sturdy enough to hold both a hanging container of soil plus the weight of the full-grown plants.

Reclaimed buckets don't have to be ugly or plain. They will last many years, so consider decorating them to match their surroundings or to stand out as artwork in their own right. You can paint; decoupage (covered with a water-proofing coat of polyurethane); wrap with brightly colored yarn, rope, or raffia; cover with fabric or contact paper; create a faux stained-glass masterpiece by gluing on a mosaic pattern from bits of glass; or whatever else your creative mind can concoct.

Another Upside-Down Option
Wire hanging baskets lined with coco fiber or sphagnum peat moss present an elegant option that also can be used year after year (change out the soil and replace the coco liner). Those with an open design in the bottom tend to allow the weight of the dirt and water to break through the lining, so look

PILES OF POTS

Stack cinder or landscape blocks *in a crisscross fashion so that empty pockets protrude at intervals. Set trailing plants in the top and let the vines cascade, or include a trellis at the back of the shelves for them to climb up.*

Create your own stacking pot sculpture *by anchoring a pipe and threading each pot over the pipe and through the hole in the bottom of the pot. Tip each pot at an angle away from the one beneath it for a planting system that only looks helter-skelter. The pots rest against each other while their weight holds them in place.*

Custom build a multilevel raised bed *that offers several sections for different types of plants.*

Build a set of shelves *against a sunny wall or corner and fill them with pots of various sizes — larger ones on the bottom row and smaller ones as you move up.*

Wire-mesh baskets lined with coco fiber make attractive upside-down planters. Look for those with crossed wire at the base.

for ones with wire crossing the bottom of the basket. To plant, line with your choice of material, gently part the liner, insert the transplant, then fill with planting medium.

TOWERS OF FLOWER (AND VEGGIE) POWER

Perhaps you've seen gardens with tires stacked neatly in piles or with strange looking wire contraptions full of dirt standing idly around. Odds are these were not junkyard gardens, but perfectly respectable plots with a conservative (as in recycling) theme. The so-called tater tower has been around a long time in several different incarnations.

The idea capitalizes on the fact that potato plants continue to develop new tubers (spuds) from stolons along the stem until just after flowering. Tower enthusiasts take advantage of this growth habit by gradually adding soil (or some other rooting medium) to the tower as the plant grows, thereby causing lots of tubers to form along its now vertical and extended stem.

The classic image is of tires piled three, four, or five high with a lush green potato plant erupting from the top of the stack. Lots of people have used this method and swear by it, but tires are made from an array of minerals and toxic substances that, given enough time, leach into the soil for your plants to soak up. While they vary from one manufacturer to the next, tires also begin to degrade in about six years, and sun exposure causes fungal dry rot. Clearly, I'm not advocating using tires in the garden. But there are plenty of substitutes!

Building a Tater Tower

Handy gardeners can design and build an attractive wooden structure to which they add slats with screws as the plants grow, increasing the height of the planter as they keep adding soil layers. Others can use a large barrel or a simple wire cylinder. In dry areas, barrels are easier to keep moist, as open-wire types may dry out too much; in damp areas, barrels can be difficult to drain properly, but an open wire design aerates nicely.

To build a wire cylinder, you'll need a 10-foot (3 m) length of 3-foot-tall (1 m) welded wire or hardware cloth. Roll it into a cylinder and attach it by bending the ends of the wire back on each other.

Your tower should be about 18 inches (46 cm) in diameter and 2 to 3 feet (61–91 cm) tall. Other materials, from bamboo fencing to large pots (5-gallon [23 L] tree pots or buckets with the bottoms removed and stacked as the

A wooden framework starts off your tater tower; as the plants grow, add another level of slats and more soil to encourage tubers to form.

plants grow), have also been used with varying degrees of success.

Once you have your structure in place, here's how to proceed.

1. Place a 6-inch (15 cm) layer of compost (or a mix of rich soil, shredded leaves, rotting straw, and organic mulch) in the bottom of the tower, then place two or three seed potatoes (whole, half, or chunks with eyes) on top.

2. Cover them with another 4-inch (10 cm) layer of compost, then water well.

3. When the sprouts reach about 6 inches tall, cover one third of the new growth (not more!) with soft soil, mulch, or compost. Keep adding layers of compost every time the sprouts reach about 6 inches tall, until the compost layers get to within about 6 inches of the top of the tower.

4. As you work your way up to the top, line each layer with black plastic, newsprint (black ink only, as colored inks can leach chemicals), or landscape fabric, both for appearance's sake and to keep the soil from falling out through the open wire.

The potato sprouts will branch out and grow over the top of the planter. The more plant growth, the more energy to feed the developing spuds. Be sure to water well, especially while the plants are in bloom, as this is when tubers are filling out. Later, when the vines yellow, your spuds are ready!

A wire tower works just as well. When it's time to harvest, just dismantle the entire structure.

Not Just for Taters

The funny thing about a potato tower is that once you try the method, you start to think of ways to adapt it to other crops. The advantage with non-tubers is that you fill up your container with dirt once, plant your seedlings up the sides and around the edges, and wait for harvesttime.

> People using the tater tower method report increased yields from 200 to 300 percent compared with field growing.

One barrel takes up a modest amount of space but might accommodate a couple of cucumber plants, some cherry tomatoes, and a zucchini. Or fill up the sides with a variety of greens and herbs and plunk a pepper plant or two on top. You could let several tomatoes dangle down the sides and plant some edible flowers or herbs on top. The possibilities are endless for creating a productive, attractive column that adds interest and flavor to any garden, balcony, or fire escape!

A large plastic barrel or garbage can with holes cut along the sides provides a sturdy structure to start with. Fill the bottom few inches with rocks or drill holes in the bottom for drainage. Or create any size container with wire mesh, lined with newspaper, coco fiber, or other permeable material that will hold the dirt in place while the plants become established. Puncture or cut slits in the liner at intervals around the tower and insert transplants into the soil. Water from the top, or consider including a drip hose inside the length of the cylinder, curling it up from the bottom up to and out the top of the tower as you fill it with soil.

A VERTICAL SALAD BAR

Greens of every sort are popular with gardeners, but most of them couldn't climb their way out of a terra-cotta pot, so they might seem out of place in a discussion of vertical gardening. But many tasty, nutritious, and versatile greens are humble little leafy plants that just happen to be ideal for growing in stacked pots, hanging baskets, and even soil walls.

Mixed garden greens can be tucked into just about any available space, helping you to really make the most of limited growing areas. Most greens are cool-season crops; that is, they will produce more tender, flavorful leaves in cool weather, but bolt (go to seed) during the height of summer. Their quick season (some leaves are harvestable in as little as three weeks) makes them ideal for succession planting, meaning you can keep the good greens coming by continuing to plant seeds or seedlings as you harvest. Summer greens may not turn out as tender or tasty as spring and fall crops, but are usually worth the gamble.

Among the greens to try are arugula (a type of mustard), chard, collards, endive, kale, varieties of red and green leaf lettuce, mustard greens, and turnip and beet greens (left to grow, they will finish into edible root crops). Be sure to wait until the danger of frost has passed to plant. Most will endure a light frost once they are established, and many people prefer the slightly sweeter flavor kale develops after a kiss of frost.

Barrels for growing greens and other goodies are available commercially, but you can make one from a standard garbage can or other large plastic barrel.

Some gardeners suggest anchoring the cylinder to the ground with rebar or a metal post driven into the ground, but on a flat surface (say, an apartment balcony where driving posts is taboo), the weight of the tower should hold it steady. Or you could anchor it with rope to a railing or other stable feature.

UP, UP, AND AWAY!

What is the future of vertical gardening? It's already here. Massive vertical urban garden structures already up and growing include a prototype system called the AlphaCrop in Cornwall, England, and a two-billion-dollar, 27-story residence in Mumbai, India, that has a four-story open garden and is billed as "the largest and tallest living wall in the world." One project in the works is Toronto's Sky-Farm, planned to jut 714 feet (218 m) into the skyline to convert just over 3 acres of prime real estate to an estimated 8 million square feet (that's close to 184 acres!) of growing space.

But are these systems practical? Are they a better use of resources than improving the methods used to farm the land already under production? Only time will tell, but it's heartening to know that creative minds are looking at the old problems of growing enough food in new and creative ways.

Among the advantages cited by proponents are:

★ Year-round crop production, with 1 indoor vertical acre equaling 4 to 6 horizontal acres outdoors (up to 30 acres for strawberries!)

★ The end of crop failure due to natural disasters such as drought, flood, and plagues of pests

★ Sustainable systems that generate their own power via solar collection and methane gas released during composting

★ All-organic growing

★ The elimination of agricultural runoff by recycling water

★ Dramatic reduction of fossil fuel consumption

★ Drastic reductions in shipping time and costs

★ Possibly ending wars over agricultural water and land usage

No measly set of goals, that.

CREATE A LIVING WALL

Where horizontal space is scarce, inventive gardeners create vertical space. Sometimes this can drive their plants right up the wall — literally. There are several ways to incorporate growing plants into your walls, indoors or out. From modular (stackable or interlocking) planters that mount to existing walls to full-scale constructed soil walls, the effect runs from decorative utility to productive magic.

Hanging wall planters are nothing new, but modular planters that fit together to cover any size and shape of wall space you fancy are a relatively recent development. **Woolly Pockets** and **Pocket Panels** are products made of recycled bottles that have been felted into a flexible, breathable fabric, then sewn into pockets and fitted with mounting hardware. Sold with fasteners and wall anchors, they are a complete, self-contained growing system.

Green Living Technologies manufactures modular stainless-steel and aluminum planters that are used to create a range of living walls (including, at 2,380 square feet [221 m²], the largest living wall in North America on the PNC Bank building in Pittsburgh, Pennsylvania).

Vertical Integration to the Nth Degree

A more ambitious approach is to build your own wall of soil, which provides tremendous vertical surface area for growing. The idea is to erect a sturdy, rigid wire frame (heavy-duty welded-wire panels work well for this), line the frame with fabric, fill it with soil mix, and plant. The walls can be devised to mount over existing walls or, with some serious engineering, can be made freestanding.

As with all container-plant gardening, maintaining soil structure integrity is a concern, so you will most likely have to deconstruct, empty, and replace the growing medium every two or three years.

Soil walls at their heart are actually large bags of soil, shaped and supported with a framework, usually made of wire mesh and a wooden frame and/or posts. Instructions for making them in a variety of sizes and configurations abound on the Internet.

PART II

Vertical

{ ANNUAL VINES }

Now that we've covered just how much better plants will fare when they grow up in the air rather than on the ground and have considered the various building materials and methods, it's time to select some plants.

A surprising variety of annual crops is suitable for growing vertically. If all you ever grow are a few single-season vines tucked into little corners of the garden, you could be feasting on scrumptious vegetables and sweet fruits all season long — and into the fall and winter if you choose to store or preserve your bounty. Get more ambitious and you could be feeding half the neighborhood.

It's no surprise that pole beans and peas are perfectly suited to this method of growing. After all, Jack didn't climb a spinach stalk! But did you know he could have? Remember, there is a variety of spinach

that climbs (see page 22). Perhaps the notion of training ground-greedy cucumbers or squash to grow up has occurred to you, but melons? No problem, if you know how to provide a little extra support.

And if you've ever seen a tomato plant flopping over the boundaries of a too-small cage, you've probably thought that there has to be a better way. There is. Free the tomatoes! Finally, would you believe there is even a root crop that will grow up? Did you guess sweet potatoes? The spuds do not rise above ground level, but the rowdy vines will enthusiastically swarm a trellis.

CHAPTER 5

BEANS

By the time Jack shinnied up the beanstalk, pole beans were already an established favorite among home gardeners. Not only are they easy to plant and grow; they also benefit the soil. Like all legumes, beans extract nitrogen from the air and convert it into a form that plant roots can absorb. This conversion is accomplished with the help of soil-dwelling microorganisms. With nitrogen being one of the three most heavily utilized elements of all green growing plants, this is no small claim to fame.

Many types of legumes are used as cover crops solely for their nitrogen-fixing ability, but anyone who has ever savored the fresh flavor of beans just plucked from the vine, lightly steamed and buttered, knows there are even more enjoyable rewards. As a group, pole beans are easy to grow and often produce bumper crops over a long season rather than in a single flush, as many bush beans do.

Beans may be used or preserved in a variety of ways with healthful, satisfying results. Pole beans, while generally bearing a little later than bush varieties, make up for their late start with extended harvest, bigger beans, and a more old-fashioned, "beany" taste.

VARIETIES

A Web search for pole beans (*Phaseolus vulgaris*) turns up nearly three million websites vying to sing their praises. They come in an almost infinite array of colors, sizes, textures, and flavors. To simplify things, we'll look at a few general categories — snap (green), French, shell, runner, Italian Rampicante (pole), lima, and asparagus (yard-long).

Snap Beans

Snap beans are also called green beans, even when they're not green. The term refers to their unripe state, not a specific color. Snap beans are harvested while the pods are narrow, smooth, and fleshy and the seeds inside are still undeveloped. The name *snap* comes from the crisp sound they make when broken in half.

Some varieties have a fibrous string running up the length of the bean, which is usually removed before eating, while others are stringless. Snap beans range from ordinary shades of green to creamy gold, mottled, or brash purple. There are many more varieties than we have room for here, but a few tried-and-true favorites deserve comment.

Stringed Varieties

BLUE LAKE (OP, 63–75 days) was once the gold standard of homegrown pole beans, especially for canning. It is stringless right up to shelling stage (see page 50). The 5- to 6-inch (15 cm) dark green pods are crisp, mild, and sweet-tasting. It is still a favorite for canning; good thing too, since it sets beans from the base of the plant to the tips of the vines in an almost continuous harvest. Other hybridized versions of Blue Lake also exist.

KENTUCKY WONDER, also called **OLD HOMESTEAD** (OP, 67 days), is one of the oldest pole bean varieties grown because it is so reliable and adaptable. It is resistant to rust and produces a tremendous harvest of 8- to 9-inch (20–23 cm) beans.

Stringless Varieties

KENTUCKY BLUE (hybrid, 58 days, AAS 1991) combines the best of Blue Lake and Kentucky Wonder. The 6- to 7-inch (15–18 cm) dark green pods are sweet and tender.

KENTUCKY WONDER WAX (OP, 65 days) produces butter yellow, 6- to 8-inch (15–20 cm) straight, almost stringless beans with fine flavor. It continues to flower until frost.

PURPLE POD POLE (OP, 67 days) looks just like you'd think. Six-foot (2 m) vines generously produce old-fashioned-tasting beans. They are easy to see for harvest and look strange enough to entice kids to eat them (though they "magically" turn green when you cook them).

French Beans

French or filet beans, also called haricots verts, are snap beans at their most delectable. Pods are harvested when they are one quarter inch (0.5 cm) or smaller in diameter.

FORTEX (OP, 70 days) is a gourmet variety. Pods are longer than most, up to 10 inches (25 cm) long, but are best picked at 6 or 7 inches (15–18 cm) for the most delicate taste and texture.

EMERITE (hybrid, 58 days) produces stringless beans that are perfection when 5 inches long, but remain exceptional up to 7 or 8 inches (18–20 cm) long. Yields of these fine-flavored beans are heavy, so pick early and often to keep the harvest coming.

Runner Beans

Runner beans grow rampant vines, often very ornamental in appearance, that can reach lengths of almost 20 feet (6 m) in a single season. The pods generally become fibrous and tough if not harvested while still quite immature.

Scarlet runner beans put on a magnificent show even before they produce a delicious crop. The beautiful blossoms attract hummingbirds.

SCARLET RUNNER BEANS (OP, 70–115 days) were cultivated as early as the 1600s. They grow quickly, reaching up to 18 feet (5.5 m) in length, and produce an abundance of beautiful scarlet flowers, followed by 8-inch-long (20 cm) beans. It is so stunning that people often grow it strictly as an ornamental, but the beans are good either as snap beans when young (about 70 days) or as shelled beans later in life (about 115 days). The more you pick the pods, the more flowers and beans keep coming.

PAINTED LADY (OP, 90 days), a variety similar to the above, dates back to 1827. Vines grow to 10 feet (3 m) long, sport scarlet and white flowers, and produce "delicious, dark brown mottled with creamy white beans," 9 to 12 inches (23–30 cm) long, according to the Burpee seed catalog. I haven't tried these yet, but that's the problem with seed catalogs: There's always something new to try!

Italian Rampicante (Pole)

Italian Rampicante (pole) or Romano beans are broad, flat, stringless, tender beans with a distinctive Old World "beany" flavor.

ROMANO ITALIAN (hybrid, 70 days) reaches 5 feet (1.5 m) tall or better, but most pods grow low on the plant. Even so, yields are generous to the point of overwhelming. The meaty green pods have the best flavor and texture when they are about 4 inches (10 cm) long.

SHELL BEANS

Shell beans, or dry beans, as the name suggests, are harvested after the seeds inside the pods have ripened and dried, and then shelled. These are the beans used in baked beans, soups, and other recipes, as well as for the seeds of the next generation. Saving your own seed to plant next year's crop works reliably only with open-pollinated (OP) varieties, which are sometimes called heirloom or heritage varieties.

One of the reasons the good ol' Kentucky Wonder bean has remained a gardener's favorite for generations is that in addition to being a favorite snap bean when harvested young, it is also a beloved shell bean when allowed to ripen on the vine. Most beans, if left on the vine to dry, can be used as shell beans.

MERAVIGLIA VENEZIA (OP, 55–60 days) sports flat, yellow, tender, stringless pods that grow to 10 inches (25 cm) or more. It is another heavy producer.

GOLDEN OF BACAU (OP, 60–70 days) produces 6- to 10-inch-long (15–25 cm), 1-inch-wide (2.5 cm), flat, golden Romano-type beans in abundance. With their remarkable sweet flavor, they are best eaten fresh but can be frozen.

MARENGO (OP, 75 days) is a bright yellow variety, with bean pods slightly larger than other types. Pods form close together, from low on the vine to the tips.

Don't eat raw runner beans and limas — they contain toxins that need to be broken down by cooking.

Lima Beans

Lima beans, also called butter beans, come in both large and "baby" types, referring to the size of the shelled seeds. The names give you some idea of what those seeds look like.

CHRISTMAS, also called Large Speckled Lima (OP, 80 days), tolerates hot weather and produces giant, healthy vines loaded with 5-inch (13 cm) pods of delicious, chestnut-flavored bean seeds.

SPECKLED CALICO (hybrid, 80 days) produces large red and white beans with scrumptious, buttery flavor.

FLORIDA SPECKLED BUTTER (OP, 85 days) has been popular since the 1840s, producing 10-foot-long (3 m) vines with clusters of bean pods, even in hot and/or humid weather. Beans are light tan with wine-colored flecks.

GIANT BEANS

For a really different harvest, try some beans that seem to have come from a fairy tale.

Asparagus or yard-long beans (OP, 70–80 days) can grow to gargantuan proportions but remain tender and tasty if picked under 18 inches (46 cm) in length. It's an old favorite partly because it is unique and partly because it is so reliable and vigorous.

A nonstop harvest of distinctly nutty-flavored, slim, stringless beans starts 70 to 80 days after planting and lasts until frost. Practically pest and disease free, the vines grow to 6 feet (2 m) long, and the beans seem as if they would too if given the chance!

KING OF THE GARDEN (OP, 88 days) grows to 5 feet (1.5 m) long and bears healthy yields of dark green, 8-inch (20 cm) pods. Each pod holds four to six large, richly flavored sweet beans.

Soybeans

Soybeans (*Glycine max*) aren't true beans, per se, but with all the health benefits ascribed to them — high in protein, fiber, and iso-flavone (believed by many to be a cancer fighter), as well as a source of calcium and B vitamins — this is as good a place as any to include them. Because they are an important commercial crop and therefore harvested by machine, breeding emphasis has been on bush varieties, so it's harder to find vining types.

Soybeans are not recommended for raw eating but instead are best baked, steamed, or even boiled. The most popular home varieties now are edamame types, which are harvested green, instead of the more traditional shelled types. Shirofumi is a favorite for home gardens as it has a sweet, nutlike taste and a smooth (not grainy) texture. Vines grow to about 3 feet (1 m) and produce in 80 to 90 days.

Soybeans grow a little differently from true beans. They tolerate heat better than most

Beans love to climb and will grow up just about anything handy, so put your fencing to work for you.

beans (except lima, which love hot weather) and handle cool spells better than lima beans. In fact, they perform best when days are warm and nights are cool. Even the bush types grow larger and floppier than standard bush beans, and will need some support.

SITE AND SOIL REQUIREMENTS

Although beans are not fussy plants, they do have their preferences. Like many cultivated plants, they like a sunny spot and moisture-retentive but well-drained soil that is rich in humus. Do not plant them where water pools after a rain. If the soil has a drainage problem, correct it by incorporating organic matter, such as peat, compost, or rotted manure, or by planting the beans in containers. Don't apply a nitrogen-heavy fertilizer unless soil tests confirm it's needed, as too much nitrogen can prompt plants to produce excess vines and leaves and fewer, later bean pods.

TRY A FEW NEW ONES

One of the many nice things about pole beans is that you can enjoy several varieties in a small area. They are self-pollinating, which means you can plant different types side by side along the same support without the plants cross-pollinating.

If you garden in a short-season area, or just want to get a jump on the season, lay black or clear plastic over well-prepared soil several weeks prior to planting to help warm the soil. Turning in half-rotted compost a few weeks before planting is another heat-generating trick.

Although beans thrive in warm weather (70°–80°F [21°C–27°C]), hot, dry spells cause them to close up shop, at least temporarily. Above 95°F (35°C), they stop flowering and may drop existing blossoms, which slows future production of beans.

PLANTING GUIDELINES

Do not plant before the soil warms, as beans simply will not germinate in cold soil. Except for fava beans, a cool-growing (mostly bush variety) cousin, beans are warmhearted. Lima beans will not ever consider germinating in soil temperatures cooler than 65°F (18°C). Even when daytime temperatures are warm, be sure all danger of frost at night is past before planting.

While a planting depth of 1 inch (2.5 cm) is commonly recommended, poking the seeds down 2 inches (5 cm) may give a little added insurance against the odd extra-cool night. Space seeds 4 to 6 inches (10–15 cm) apart along a fence or A-frame trellis, or in groups of four or five at each foot of a tepee trellis. You will be thinning as the plants progress.

Be sure to leave enough room between rows or groups for you to work without catching or damaging the vines. Press the soil down gently but firmly, and soak it to be sure each seed has good contact with the moist soil.

> Brand-new bean seedlings may need to be placed against their support, but once they latch on, they are on their way.

If you prewarmed the soil with plastic, you can remove it at planting time or leave it in place as an inorganic mulch. Just plant right through it by cutting an X every 6 inches (15 cm) and pushing two seeds into the soil through each slit.

Plant lima bean seeds with the eye facing down. The first roots will emerge from here and will orient the young plants in the right direction.

GIVE YOUR BEANS THEIR BEST SHOT

One of the best things that you can do for your bean crop, especially if you are planting in a spot where no legumes have grown before, is to inoculate the seeds. The soft black powder inoculate actually comprises thousands of microbes that convert nitrogen from a gas into a plant-usable form. Since some soils may be lacking in these organisms, it is prudent to ensure their presence by pretreating your seeds. The inoculate is available online, at garden outlets, or through mail-order catalogs.

Treating seeds is quick and easy. Soak seeds for a few hours or overnight the night before you intend to plant. Drain off excess water. Empty the contents of the inoculate packet into a jar or sealable plastic bag; toss in the now plumped-up, damp seeds; and gently shake the bag until the seeds are well coated. Proceed to plant!

Plant soybeans about 2 inches (5 cm) deep, spaced 4 to 5 inches (10–12 cm) apart, in rows about 2 feet (61 cm) apart. Be sure they are situated so they aren't shaded by other plants or trellises.

Presprouting

Pole bean seeds germinate in 7 to 14 days, or sooner if presprouted. Presprouting may help you get a jump on a short growing season. Place bean seeds in a wet coffee filter or paper towel. Fold and place it in a plastic bag and let sit in windowsill for two days. Check carefully for roots to emerge. The germinating seeds must be handled with extreme care because any damage or bruising will injure the infant plants. As soon as the seeds have sprouted, follow outdoor planting directions.

Don't wait until they develop long roots, as the plants will consider that a form of transplanting. Beans detest transplanting. So don't bother to start beans indoors or waste your money on transplant seedlings. They will express their displeasure by growing into weak plants with sad harvests.

TRAINING BEANS TO GROW UP

Beans will twine around anything! Ten-foot (3 m) bean poles driven into the soil have long been a common sight in backyard gardens, but there are many other ways to support them. I knew a family who transformed an old swing set into a bean trellis and trained pole beans up the frame of an old playhouse!

Tepee trellises are a popular method for training pole beans. Especially in windy areas, it is a good idea to push the bottom end of the poles into the prepared soil for stability. Starting with the tripod described on page 20, position the poles in a 3-, 4-, or 5-foot-wide (1–2 m) circle, then add more poles until there

An old swing set is given a new lease on life to support bean vines.

are 6 to 12 inches (15–30 cm) between the feet. One to three vines can climb each leg of the tepee. A running tepee is also superb for pole beans. Again, space the feet of the poles 6 to 12 inches (15–30 cm) apart.

Just about any style of trellis with lots of narrow, vertical components (plant supports) works for beans. Twine or wire supports serve equally well on a fence or an A-frame. The slight slant of the A-frame allows the beans to hang down away from the foliage, which makes them a snap to pick from underneath. Commercial bean towers work fine if you use every other strand; otherwise they tend to crowd the vines (see the next page).

The most important thing to consider when choosing a trellis for pole beans is that it is tall and sturdy enough for the variety you are growing. It is also important to have the trellis ready before you plant. Any poles or posts that extend beneath the soil line should go into the ground before the seeds do. Otherwise, you may accidentally damage tender seedling roots if you don't get around to putting them in until later. In my garden, "later" is already overbooked!

Beans do not like to be overcrowded; they need ample space for roots and foliage to spread out and for adequate ventilation around foliage. Once the young plants have become established, thin them to the best two or three per pole or no more than one vine every 6 inches (15 cm) along a fence. Never pull up the castoffs; their roots may be intertwined with their neighbors. Instead, snip them off near the soil level with scissors to avoid disturbing other plant roots.

Weed with care to avoid damaging those delicate roots. Cultivate shallowly since the feeder roots are near the surface. Putting down a 4-inch (10 cm) layer of mulch after the seedlings have grown a foot (30 cm) or so tall will significantly cut down on weeding and will also help keep the roots cool and moist.

THE THREE SISTERS

The traditional bean supports used by homesteaders and Native Americans were cornstalks. Grown with squash, this method is known as the Three Sisters Garden, a method of interplanting, or companion planting, that benefits all three plants. Corn provides support, squash shades the ground, and beans feed the soil. There are many configurations — from planting in flat soil, to multiple soil mounds, to one big mound, but the concept is the same. Here's one example:

★ After all danger of frost has past, prepare a 6- to 8-foot (2–2.5 m) area, preferably mounded.

★ First plant corn seeds in the center of the mound (10 to 16 seeds, spaced about 12 inches (30 cm) apart, two seeds per planting hole). After the seeds sprout, thin to one stalk per hole.

★ Once the corn reaches about 6 inches (15 cm) high, mound a few inches (about 8 cm) of soil around the base of each plant. This extra soil helps further stabilize the plants and serves as the planting medium for the beans.

★ Next, plant two to four bean seeds around each corn plant, about 3 inches from the stalks.

★ As soon as the bean plants come up, plant two or three vining squash around the perimeter of the beans, 1 or 2 feet (30–61 cm) apart.

★ Thin to one squash plant for every 3 square feet of space.

★ Guide the growing bean vines up the cornstalks, and occasionally check and guide the squash vines to cover the mound.

CHAPTER 6

PEAS

Oh, how gardeners need peas. Peas (*Pisum sativum*) are among the first seeds to be planted in the garden in the spring. Within just a few weeks, their energetic growth, delightful early flowers, and succulent, sweet pods reward the gardener for getting an early start, often during those so-called spring days when the weather is still cold and dreary, and the motivation to be outdoors is low.

Not only do they reward your earliest efforts directly with tasty and abundant crops, but peas also benefit the gardener by more indirect means. Like all legumes, peas, through nodules in their root system, fix nitrogen into the soil by converting it from atmospheric gas into a form usable by plants.

VARIETIES
Peas differ greatly in growth habit, pod formation, and days to maturity. While many pea vines reach for the sky, merrily scaling 6-foot (2 m) trellises, some dwarf varieties stop short, reaching only 24 to 30 inches (51–76 cm) tall. Tall types need a good solid framework to grow up lest they sprawl into a tangle, and even dwarf varieties benefit from a structural support.

Pod types include English (also called garden or shelling peas), which are shelled to be eaten; snap peas, which are eaten pod and all; and snow peas, which are eaten while the pods are flat and immature. Differing days to maturity allows you to plant several types to extend the harvest all season long. With so many varieties available, consider the following descriptions as only a small sampler of your choices.

Shelling Peas

Shelling peas come in both tall and dwarf varieties. Like shelling beans, they are grown until the peas are fully formed in the pods, then harvested, shelled, and cooked before eating. Unlike beans, they are not left on the vine to dry.

ALDERMAN, also called **Tall Telephone** (OP, 85 days), is a late-maturing variety, best known for huge, easy shelling pods that hold six to eight fine-flavored peas each. It grows 6 to 8 feet (2–2.5 m) tall and matures in 85 days for a late-season harvest.

LINCOLN, also called **Homesteader** (OP, 66 days), grows reliably even as the weather heats up. Three-foot-long (1 m) vines produce smallish pods, about 3 inches (8 cm) long, packed with nine small, ultra-sweet peas apiece. This variety is highly recommended for freezing.

WANDO (hybrid, 68 days) is another heat-tolerant, late-maturing variety, touted for its versatility whether used fresh, canned, or frozen. It matures with six to eight medium-sized peas per pod.

ECLIPSE (hybrid, 67 days) is hailed as "the world's first super-sweet pea," owing to its high sugar content — 20 to 30 percent more than other varieties. Harvest lasts longer than with many other varieties, as these peas hold their sugar content exceptionally well. Eclipse is resistant to powdery mildew.

MR. BIG (hybrid, 58–62 days) was a 2000 AAS winner. It grows well throughout the United States, yielding 4- to 6-inch (10–15 cm) pods of six to ten sweet-tasting peas each. Vines grow only 2 to 3 feet long (0.5–1 m) but still need trellising for support. Picked peas stay sweet and tender longer than most others.

MAESTRO (OP, 60 days) is the shortest of the group, growing up to only 22 inches (56 cm) tall. It offers long, narrow pods of eight or nine sweet, tender peas starting in just 60 days over an extended period of harvest. It is resistant to powdery mildew and enation (a viral infection).

To save seeds (only possible with open-pollinated varieties), leave some pods until they become very full and lumpy, with a rough, dull green skin.

Snap Peas

Snap peas, sometimes called sugar snap peas, are the result of crossing shelling peas with snow peas. They have the plump shape of the former and the sweet flavor of the latter. Some varieties have a fibrous string running the length of the pods, but the entire pod can be eaten. Dwarf and tall vining varieties are available.

SUGAR SNAP (OP, 70 days), an AAS winner, is the original Sugar Snap variety, and as new and improved varieties abound, it is getting harder to find. Vines grow to 6 feet (1.8 m) and require strong support. Peas are about 3 inches (7.6 cm) long, well filled, and sweetly delicious. Multiple plantings, 7 to 10 days apart, are recommended for extended harvest.

SUPER SUGAR SNAP (OP, 58 days) usurps its predecessor's reputation as it sets fuller fruit, about a week earlier in the season, and yields bigger harvests, all with improved disease resistance.

SUGAR SPRINT (OP, 61 days) produces quickly, offering up heavy yields over an extended harvest due to its heat tolerance and resistance to powdery mildew and pea enation. Vines grow only 24 to 30 inches (61–76 cm) long.

CASCADIA (OP, 48–60 days) is an exceptionally early producer. Like Sugar Sprint, it is resistant to pea enation and powdery mildew and sets a thick harvest on compact, 32-inch (81 cm) vines.

Snow Peas

Snow peas are those wide, flat pods that are most familiar to nongardeners as a typical

ingredient in Chinese food. Always eaten whole, they have a sweet, delicate taste and a tender, crisp texture.

OREGON SUGAR POD II (OP, 65 days) is a long-time favorite that sets bountiful crops on short (30 inch [76 cm]) vines. It is among the easiest to grow, as it is highly disease resistant.

GOLIATH (OP, 60 days, AAS 2003) offers bountiful yields of sweet, tender, stringless peas on vines up to 5 feet (1.5 m) long.

SANDY (OP, 75 days) is a fairly new introduction. Its 3½- to 4-foot-long (1–1.5 m) vines produce more than the usual amount of coiling tendrils, a delicacy served steamed in various Asian dishes.

Like other legumes, peas improve the soil by fixing nitrogen into it.

MAMMOTH MELTING SUGAR (OP, 65 days) erupts in vigorous vines that quickly swarm to about 5 feet (2.5 m) in length. Pods have a unique, sweet, delicate taste that melts in the mouth. Stringless pods just keep on coming the more you pick them.

SITE AND SOIL REQUIREMENTS

Although peas need full sun early in the season, they appreciate partial shade during the summer. All varieties can tolerate frost, but few do well in hot weather. Though some varieties are more heat tolerant than others, peas are cool-season plants and will not flower or set fruit in very hot weather.

Peas do not require especially fertile ground. They do well in just about anything but heavy clay. A little compost or aged manure at planting time should supply all the nutrients that are needed for the plants to get off to a good start.

Phosphorus or potash deficiency can cause leaves to curl or turn purple. Wood ashes (5 to 10 pounds [2–4 kg] per 100 square feet [30 m²]) will provide both of these nutrients. Ashes also serve to buffer extremely acid soils. Peas do best in a pH range of 5.5 to 7.5.

Well-drained soil is essential to healthy pea vines. Plants take in oxygen through their roots, and soggy soil can deprive them of as much as 90 percent of the oxygen that they need. It also interferes with the plant's ability to take up nitrogen. Soils rich in organic matter are pea heaven not only because of the improved drainage, but also because of a healthy nutrient content. Lighten clay by working in compost, peat, or other organic matter.

....

Stagger planting over several weeks to yield a harvest over a prolonged season, or plant early-, midseason-, and late-ripening varieties.

....

PLANTING GUIDELINES

Peas generally do not take well to transplanting. If you can't resist the urge, start them indoors in peat pots and set them out, pots and all. But there is little to be gained with this method. You're better off preparing your site the previous fall so you can direct-seed at the earliest possible opportunity. Germination takes 7 to 14 days in soil temperatures of 40°F (4°C) or warmer.

On the day before planting, soak the peas overnight in warm water to relax the tough seed coat. Soaking plumps up the dehydrated seeds and helps to speed germination. It also makes them more receptive to inoculate (see "Give Your Beans Their Best Shot," page 53).

Plant the seeds 2 inches (5 cm) deep in heavy or warmed soil, or 1 inch (2.5 cm) deep in lighter or still cool (not frozen) ground. Peas enjoy their own company and do well when they are crowded. There are two ways to take advantage of this for a space-saving garden.

One is to crowd lower-growing varieties together in wide beds and support the entire bed with a zigzag twine support (see page 27). The plants will crowd out weeds, shade each others' roots, and lean on one another for

NOT JUST A SPRING FASHION

Fall pea crops are a mixed bag, iffy but possible. Plant a fall crop 60 to 70 days before the first expected autumn frost. You may have to coddle the young seedlings in the heat of summer, and often heat stress or powdery mildew will ruin the crop before it flowers. But in areas without extreme heat, or in a lucky year, a bounty of fall peas is a welcome treat.

support, all while producing record numbers of peas per square foot.

A more intensive ground-saving method is to plant them in double rows, spaced 3 inches (8 cm) apart each way along a pea fence or trellis.

TRAINING PEAS TO GROW UP

Many varieties of pea vines are enthusiastic climbers that easily top heights of 6 feet (2 m). Grasping, coiling tendrils anchor the vines to any stationary support, including each other and slow-moving gardeners.

The type of trellis depends on whether you are growing standard or dwarf varieties. Even the shortest vines will flop into a tangled mass without some type of support. Two-foot-tall (0.5 m) pea fences, or even just branches pushed into the soil alongside the plants, will take care of the dwarfs, but the taller-growing varieties need a more substantial support. A pea trellis must be tall enough to accommodate the length of the vines, which will produce fruit all the way to their tops.

Vertical fences made of wire mesh or rows of twine strung either vertically or horizontally work well, though vines will need occasional guidance to find their way from one horizontal "rung" to the next. Similarly constructed A-frames are perfect for peas because two double rows can be grown side by side. Tepees are also good pea trellises (see pages 20–23).

Until the vines find the plant support, they may need a little help. Lean the young vines into the support material, perhaps by weaving the tips of the vines among the strands. Once the tendrils contact the support, they will coil around tightly as the vine continues to grow upward. No tying or additional support is necessary.

Peas are very hardy in that they grow vigorously, can withstand frost, and are fairly drought tolerant, but they cannot take the heat. Early planting is a must. The seeds must be kept moist to germinate, but once they sprout, they require surprisingly little water until they flower. At this point, 1 inch (2.5 cm) of water per week will suffice.

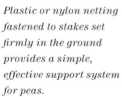

Plastic or nylon netting fastened to stakes set firmly in the ground provides a simple, effective support system for peas.

CHAPTER 7

TOMATOES

The vegetable (I know, I know, it's really a fruit) we now consider a staple in pasta sauces, chili, and countless other dishes was once believed to be as deadly as its close relative, belladonna. Their flowers are quite similar, but the fruits are distinctly different, especially in that tomatoes won't kill you. To indulge in the succulent red flesh was to flirt with death. Surely only fools or witches would dare the tempting fruit, which some think was the original apple of Eden.

Natives of the New World, however, had long enjoyed the refreshing taste of tomatoes, and once suspicious settlers overcame their skepticism and sometimes outright dread, they soon found themselves sharing the bounty of the ruddy harvest. Today the tomato stands out as the king of the home garden vegetables — the single most popular plant grown. Here are some tips on producing the best tomatoes you've ever tasted!

TO~MAY~TOE, TO~MAH~TOE

There's more going on here than mere pronunciation. Aside from its early mistaken-identity crisis as a poisonous plant, this household favorite has endured more name changes than a marriage-minded gold-digger. Originally classified as *Lycopersicon* (translation: wolf peach), it was later reclassified as *Solanum* (the nightshade family), then finally reassigned the genus *Lycopersicon*, species *esculentum* or *lycopersicon*. So you are apt to find it listed botanically under more than one Latin name.

And just to keep things complicated, there is an entirely separate species (see Currant Tomatoes on page 63) that readily cross-pollinates with its cousins. Toxic relatives, dodgy name changes, and promiscuous cousins — no wonder the tomato blushes!

HOW DOES YOUR TOMATO GROW?

The distinction between indeterminate and determinate tomatoes is one of growth habit. **Indeterminate** tomatoes continue to grow, flower, and fruit until killed by frost. The vines can grow 6 feet (2 m) long or more given ideal conditions. They usually ripen large fruit late in the season.

Determinate varieties grow until they reach their genetically determined limit, regardless of the best conditions. The vine ends in a cluster of flowers and will grow no further. These generally produce early, smaller fruit over a limited harvesttime of 4 to 6 weeks. Something of a cross between the two, **indeterminate short internode** (ISI) varieties have the shorter growth habit of a determinate variety but can fruit continuously like indeterminate varieties. Almost all heritage, or open-pollinated, varieties are indeterminate, usually making them the first choice for training to grow up.

VARIETIES

The diversity in tomato cultivars is staggering. Varieties can be open-pollinated or hybrid; indeterminate or determinate; and early, mid-season, or late fruiting. They also produce fruit in a bewildering variety of shapes, sizes, and colors. Some tomatoes are hollow; some thick and meaty. Some have inbred resistance to diseases and pests. There are even notable differences in nutritive values.

Although not outwardly evident, the most important advances in tomato breeding are those of disease resistance. The devastating effects of many common tomato diseases can be easily avoided simply by planting disease-resistant varieties. Celebrity Hybrid, for example, is noted for strong plants that are resistant to fusarium wilts (I and II) and verticillium wilt, tobacco mosaic virus, and nematodes.

No matter what the color, shape, or season in which a tomato ripens, the bottom line is taste. As you scan those brilliantly illustrated pages of seed catalogs and websites, note what attribute is mentioned first under each entry. If the color, size, growth habit, shape, earliness, or disease resistance is the most notable aspect of any given variety, that is what the entries will list. But if the flavor is outstanding, they will say so right up front.

Short-Season Varieties

Early-fruiting or short-season varieties are popular with northern gardeners and with anyone who wants to get a jump on the season. Generally, they tend to produce smallish fruit (average about 4 ounces [113 g]) with so-so flavor on smaller, denser plants. For some gardeners, the choice between early (or in some areas, any) tomatoes and minimal space–taking vines can be a real conundrum. Some varieties can produce mature fruit in as little as 45 days from transplanting, a decent trade-off for the extra bit of ground space they require over more vertically inclined varieties.

SIBERIAN (OP, 48–60 days, determinate) is an heirloom variety from Russia. Its 2- to 3-inch (5–8 cm) fruit, which sets in temperatures as low as 38°F (3°C), has strong tomato flavor and an oval shape that is excellent for canning.

The smaller varieties of tomatoes, with their gorgeous colors, vibrant flavors, and abundant crops, can be grown just about anywhere and are happy to share their space with other veggies.

SANTIAM (OP, 60 days, determinate, VF) and **OREGON SPRING** (OP, 70 days, determinate) are similar to the above, having been developed at Oregon State University to endure those cool, damp springs. Oregon Spring can go out in the garden a month before last frost, with protection only on frosty nights. Santiam produces earlier and is also disease resistant.

STUPICE (OP, 60–65 days) may be the best bet to train up as it produces all season on indeterminate vines, giving you not only an early start, but also an extended finish. Fruit is small (2 inches [5 cm] in diameter) and tasty.

Fruit-Shaped Fruits

Tomatoes come in almost as many shapes and sizes as gardeners do! Some are tiny. Some are huge. Some are round and full, others elongated, and several varieties are shaped like different fruits.

Currant Tomatoes

Currant tomatoes (65–68 days, indeterminate, unless otherwise noted) are the tiniest, most flavor-packed tomatoes you can grow. Pretty enough to be planted as ornamentals, these prolific plants produce sprays of tiny, sweet-tart, tasty tomatoes. The vines tend to sprawl, but training and pinching back to control growth will keep them in order.

Although a different species from most tomato varieties, they cross-pollinate readily, so grow them well away from other types if you intend to save seed. Up to 10 percent of the plants grown from saved seed will produce yellow fruit. Though often sold simply as generic red currant tomatoes, there are also named varieties.

WORTH LOOKING FOR

Disease resistance in plants is of such extreme importance that it is usually noted by an abbreviation in the names of such varieties. Look for names such as Hybrid Gurney Girl VFNT. Disease resistance in tomatoes is signified by these abbreviations:

F1	Fusarium wilt race 1
F2	Fusarium wilt race 2
F3	Fusarium wilt race 3
N	Root-knot nematodes (tiny soil-borne pests)
T	Tobacco mosaic virus
V	Verticillium wilt (soilborne fungal disease)
A	*Alternaria alternata* (crown wilt)
L	Leafspot (septoria)
St	Stempylium (gray leaf spot)

HAWAIIAN CURRANT (OP, 79 days). Pea-sized fruit is red, sweet, and borne on clusters that hold the fruits until each is ripe.

MATT'S WILD CHERRY CURRANT (OP, 70 days). So easy to grow, it self-sows! This is the wild species, which means it grows like a weed. Highly sweet and plentiful, the fruit is about the size of small marbles.

CERISE ORANGE (OP, 75 days). Sweet, low-acid, ½-inch (1 cm) fruit crowds the vines until frost.

BLONDKOPFCHEN (OP, 75 days). German for "little blonde girl," this variety bears sparkling, ½-inch (1 cm), bright yellow tomatoes in clusters of up to 30. They are scrumptiously sweet with a citrusy aftertaste. Crack- and disease-resistant, they grow well even in cool areas.

Grape Tomatoes

Grape tomatoes first became available in specialty food shops in the late 1990s and have since become so popular that they have all but replaced cherry tomatoes (see below) on grocery shelves. Intensely sweet, with thicker skin, meatier flesh, and less water content than cherry types, grape tomatoes produce ½- to ¾-inch (1–2 cm) grapelike fruits.

Varieties sold as Grape or Red Grape Hybrid are highly disease resistant and heat tolerant, producing long clusters of 24 fruits each as early as 60 days from transplanting.

RIESENTRAUBE (OP, 70 days, indeterminate) is German for a "giant bunch of grapes," and that's just how they look and not far from how they taste. Sweet clusters decorate the vines throughout the season.

SUGAR PLUM F1 (hybrid, 67 days, indeterminate) is incredibly sweet, routinely beating out other varieties in taste tests. Long, easy-to-harvest clusters of deep red, 1-inch (2.5 cm) fruit weigh down the vines with heavy harvests.

SWEET HEARTS F1 (hybrid, 70 days, indeterminate) is very sweet, with an excellent shelf life for storage. It boasts massive yields of bright red, uniformly shaped, superb-flavored fruit that is resistant to cracking, TMV, and fusarium wilt I.

JULIET (hybrid, 60 days, indeterminate, 1999 AAS Winner) sports clusters of sweet, red, elongated, crack-resistant fruits, about 1 ounce (28 g) each.

Cherry Tomatoes

Cherry tomatoes still enjoy a favorite spot in many home gardens. The reason they suffered commercially compared to grape tomatoes is that their thinner skin tends to bruise more in shipping. They are easy to grow and so sweet to eat!

SUPER SWEET 100 VF (hybrid, 65 days, indeterminate) takes over where the old Sweet 100 variety left off. Incredibly productive and vigorous, plants yield sweet, 1-inch (2.5 cm), vitamin C–packed tomatoes throughout the season. The vines ramble, so tie early and tie often.

SWEET MILLION VFT (hybrid, 60 days, indeterminate) offers even better disease resistance and productivity, producing mouthwatering 1- to 1½-inch (2.5–4 cm) fruit right until frost.

COYOTE (OP, 50 days, indeterminate) is a wild native of Mexico that produces tons of tiny, translucent yellow tomatoes with outstanding flavor.

RED PEAR (OP, 70 days, indeterminate), like its near kin **YELLOW PEAR** (OP, 78 days, indeterminate), offers unusual pear-shaped, mild-flavored, and firm fruit. Saved Yellow Pear seeds have proved viable after

18 years, and the plants are often the last surviving producers in the fall.

SUGARY (hybrid, 80 days, semi-determinate, 2005 AAS Winner) produces juicy, 2-ounce (56 g), super-sweet red tomatoes that consistently win growing and taste tests.

Plum Tomatoes

Plum or paste tomatoes are familiar to good cooks everywhere as sauce tomatoes. Their meaty texture and low water content make them ideal for cooking down, as they take a lot less time than do juicier varieties.

ROMA VFA (hybrid, 75 days, determinate) is the classic paste tomato, offering heavy yields of bright red, thick-fleshed fruit with few seeds.

AMISH PASTE (OP, 74 days, indeterminate) is somewhat lower in acid but high in classic tomato flavor. Fruit is deep red, meaty, and about 8 ounces (226 g) on average.

SUPER MARZANO (hybrid, 85 days, indeterminate) is an upgrade of the classic Marzano, with superior disease resistance and outstanding, vigorous production of rich, red,

5-inch-long (13 cm) tomatoes. The fruit is high in pectin for naturally thick, creamy sauces.

BLACK PLUM (OP, 80 days, indeterminate) tomatoes aren't particularly attractive to look at, but oh, that sweet, dense flesh. They not only sauce superbly, but also dry and slice with the best of 'em. The 2- to 4-ounce (56 to 113 g) fruit is a muddy brown (not black) when ripe, borne on 6-foot-long (2 m) vines.

The Big Boys (and Girls)

The main season and slicing varieties are those probably familiar to most home gardeners — or those who live next door to most home gardeners. The categories are a tad misleading, as many can be early, midseason, or late, and most are certainly good for a variety of purposes beyond slicing. But it is that slab of red, ripe, juicy tomato, picked fresh from the garden and positioned reverently on a bun or sandwich, or devoured with a sprinkle of salt and pepper, that has endeared the tomato forever to our hearts.

TAKE THIS TOMATO AND STUFF IT

Stuffing tomatoes come in a range of shapes and colors but are somewhat limited in taste. Most are shaped more like bell peppers than tomatoes and are almost hollow to match. Lop off the top, and you'll find a mass of seeds beneath the stem that scoops out neatly, leaving a nice vacancy for your choice of stuffing.

Yellow Stuffer (OP, 85 days, indeterminate) is the most widely available variety. Hollow, except for the occasional rib similar to that of the bell peppers they mimic, the thick tomato walls are perfect for an edible bowl.

Schimmeig Striped Hollow (OP, 80 days, indeterminate) is prolific, churning out loads of 3- to 5-inch (8–13 cm) gold- and red-striped fruit on relatively short (30 inch [76 cm]) vines.

BETTER BOY VF1NAST (hybrid, 70 days, AAS Winner) offers deep red, flavorful, juicy tomatoes that can top a full pound (0.5 kg). Grows nearly anywhere.

CELEBRITY VF1F2NTAST (hybrid, 70 days, 1984 AAS Winner). I grow this tomato every year because I know I can! With its excellent flavor in abundant 8-ounce (226 g) red fruits, this one never lets you down.

CHAMPION VFNT and **CHAMPION II VFFNTA** (hybrid, 62–64 days, indeterminate) are two versions of the sweetest, meatiest, most luscious tomatoes you can grow. Fruits are 6 to 8 ounces (170–226 g) and very abundant.

BRANDYWINE (OP, 95 days, indeterminate) is an Amish heirloom that has withstood the taste tests of time. Considered by many to be the best-tasting tomato of all time, it is always a contender — large, juicy, and yummy!

Best Bets for Baskets

Some vines just naturally lend themselves to trailing as much or more than growing up. As long as they gobble up vertical space, they qualify as growing up even if they technically grow down. Here are a few suggestions:

SWEET PEA (OP, 62 days, indeterminate, currant type). Delectable, itty-bitty bites of ruby red, sweet, currantlike flavor load the trailing vines.

RED CHERRY (OP, 65 days, indeterminate, cherry type). Flavorful, small, pinkish red oval fruit grows on dense, trailing plants.

GOLDEN RAVE FT (hybrid, 67 days, indeterminate). Sweet like a grape tomato, meaty like a Roma, with 2-inch (5 cm) fruit, this variety represents a whole new type, the Romanito. It thrives in a range of climates and resists cracking.

TUMBLING TOM SERIES (hybrid, 70 days, indeterminate). Red and yellow strains make an attractive, ornamental hanging basket with sweet, 1- to 2-inch (2.5–5 cm) fruit.

Creative Colors

Although bright red tomatoes make the mouth water with anticipation, they are only the beginning of the rainbow. Gorgeously colored varieties offer something special for the growing-up garden, in terms of both visual appeal and epicurean taste.

SUPER SNOW WHITE (OP, 75 days, indeterminate) produces low-acid fruit about the size and color of a Ping Pong ball.

WHITE POTATO LEAF, also sold as **Shah, Mikado White,** or **White Brandywine** (OP, 75 days, indeterminate), produces 3- to 6-ounce (85–170 g) almost ghostly white fruit.

LEMON BOY (hybrid, 72 days, determinate) is a favorite for its pure lemon yellow color, mild flavor, and reliable growing habit.

SUN GOLD (hybrid, 55 days, indeterminate) produces bountiful harvests of rich, golden-colored, sweetly flavored cherry tomatoes.

MOONGLOW (OP, 85 days, indeterminate) is one of the best orange tomatoes for flavor and texture. Fruit is 6 to 8 ounces (170–226 g).

CHEROKEE PURPLE (OP, 85 days, indeterminate) tolerates mild drought and many common diseases. This heirloom from

Tennessee is ugly and keeps poorly, but it tastes absolutely wonderful.

BLACK CHERRY (OP, 64 days, indeterminate) is more of a deep purple-brown, but the fruit is sweet with rich, layered flavors that burst in your mouth.

Don't plant tomatoes or related crops, such as peppers or eggplant, in the same area more than once every three years (see Rule No. 8, Page 10).

FOCUS ON NUTRITION

Some differences in fruit, however, are not as obvious as size, color, flesh, or shape. Though all tomatoes are high in vitamin C when raw and lycopene when cooked, a few offer additional benefits in terms of nutritional value.

HIGH CAROTENE (OP, 76 days, indeterminate) tomatoes have more than twice the carotene level of other varieties. The vines need good support.

DOUBLE RICH (OP, 65–70 days, indeterminate) produces 3-inch (8 cm) fruit with twice the normal levels of vitamin C in a plant that is itself disease resistant. Is there a connection? Could be!

LONG KEEPER (hybrid, 78 days, semi-determinate) is still the pick for those who want to store tomatoes for two, three, or even four months by simply placing them on a shelf at 65°F (18°C). (No need to wrap them, but be sure they don't touch one another.) They won't taste garden fresh, but they'll rival anything you can bring home from the grocery store.

SITE AND SOIL REQUIREMENTS

Tomatoes demand only the best. It takes lots of sunshine and a well-drained soil rich in organic matter and well-balanced nutrients to keep them happy. They prefer a fairly acid soil with a pH from 5.5 to 6.5. Try arranging

TRY A TOMATILLO!

Not quite a tomato but grown the same way, tomatillos are a staple in Mexican dishes and an attractive addition to any garden.

Tomatillos (*Physalis philadelphica*), also called ground cherries, Mexican tomatoes, and husk tomatoes, are a not-too-distant cousin of the Solanaceae family. The flowers look like typical nightshade family flowers. As the fruit begins to form, paperlike husks develop that look like little lanterns adorning the vining stems. The mature fruit is either green, yellowish, or purple, depending on the variety, still wearing that protective husk.

Grown and trellised like tomatoes, tomatillos are practically pest- and disease-free and will readily self-sow. They prosper in any climate. Direct-sow in many areas after all danger of frost is past, or start indoors and transplant as for tomatoes.

Harvest when still green and tangy by gently pulling the fruit free from the vine, as the plant will continue to produce throughout the season. Leave the husks on until ready to use. They will keep in the fridge for up to four weeks and can even be frozen. Blend some up into a tasty green salsa verde and enjoy!

trained tomatoes around the base of a compost pile for healthy, carefree plants. Or give them a few feedings over the season with fish emulsion. You can work compost into the soil near the roots any time after the tomatoes begin to flower; just be very careful around shallow feeder roots.

As the growing season wanes, pinch off new flowers so that the plants will concentrate on ripening the fruit that has already set.

Be wary about fertilizing. Tomatoes despise imbalances in nutrients and are quick to tattle about any deficiencies or excesses, which makes these plants prime indicators of soil condition. For instance, too much nitrogen in the soil produces lots of vine and little fruit. A little bonemeal or colloidal phosphate, added to the soil at planting time, helps balance nitrogen content and encourages strong, healthy plants.

Water Warning

Erratic watering wreaks havoc on tomatoes. A dry spell that is followed by a soaking causes the fruit to crack and leaves it vulnerable to decay. The soil around tomatoes should never be allowed to dry out entirely, nor should their roots be constantly wet. (Some varieties prefer a little drying between watering, so be sure to read catalog descriptions carefully.)

Keep plants evenly moist — not drenched — to prevent sudden shifts in the available water supply as the plants grow. To force ripening all at once, stop watering. As the soil dries out, the plants are stressed

EXTEND THE SEASON

Most tomatoes are very cold sensitive, so use the added benefit of the support framework for cold protection. Whenever cold weather threatens, simply drape plastic sheeting, sheets, or a light blanket over whatever system you've chosen.

Frost protection can make all the difference between a long, productive season and skimpy plants with a few green tomatoes. Just as early-frost protection gets young seedlings off to a good start, loaded vines have a much better chance of yielding ripe fruit if you are ready with some covers on that first freezing night. Often a cold snap is followed by days or even weeks of sunny, fruit-ripening weather. Be prepared.

and soon come to realize that the end is near, which causes them to focus their energy into ripening their species' perpetuating fruit. The best time to do this, in most areas, is mid- to late summer.

PLANTING GUIDELINES

There's no shame in using seedlings from a nursery to get your garden growing, but doing so limits your selection. Starting your own seedlings allows you to experiment with a wider range of varieties, including many heirloom plants that might be hard to find at your local nursery.

Tomato seedlings have a few basic needs that must be met as soon as they sprout. Strong, even lighting will help them grow stout and green. Hang grow-lights (fluorescent lights will do just as well for transplants)

TOMATOES
IN POTS

If you are really short on space and/ or growing season, consider growing tomatoes in containers. Large containers will host tomatoes quite nicely; just be sure to water often (up to several times a day) and to feed with a liquid fertilizer throughout the season, as the roots won't be able to forage for themselves. Bags, pouches, hanging baskets, and planter boxes are all available for tomatoes and all help make use of vertical space whether the vines climb upward or dangle. (See also page 39.)

Containers help extend the season because if the weather cools down too much, you can just haul them back indoors until it warms back up. If you are staking your container tomatoes, be sure to use a container deep enough to support a stake; about 2 feet (61 cm) is minimum. You can also rest a freestanding cage or even an old A-frame-style clothes-drying rack over the container as a support system.

as close to the tops of the plants as you can without touching, or keep plants on a table by a sunny window and turn them two or three times a day to prevent lopsided growth.

Determinate tomatoes should not be pruned because removing any of their branches reduces yield.

The seedlings also need room to grow healthy roots. Unlike some other transplants, tomatoes thrive when repotted. The secret is to graduate to increasingly deeper containers for each repotting, so plan on repotting at least once before transplanting into the garden. To repot, remove all but the top few leaves, set the seedling deeper into the new soil than it grew previously, and carefully bury it up to the leaves.

The stem will send out more roots along the buried portion. Those extra roots help to produce stronger, stockier, more vigorous seedlings than those grown in their original container. Keep the soil moist and temperature above 50°F (10°C) for the best growth. Overly warm temperatures and insufficient light, common problems for plants started indoors, produce tall, spindly, pale plants.

A week or so before you move your seedlings outside, begin to harden them off (see Appendix 4). This step is critical in successfully transplanting your carefully tended seedlings. Dig holes deep enough that you can set the young tomatoes in deeper than they were growing in their containers. Prune all but the top few sets of leaves, then bury the plant to within 3 inches (8 cm) of the top. Besides forcing new roots, this reduces moisture loss through the leaves, a common cause of transplant stress. Water well and keep evenly moist.

Maybe you're a stickler for perfect-looking tomatoes, maybe not, but especially for stuffing tomatoes, where presentation is important, smooth, unblemished skin is the perfect finishing touch. While even watering is essential to prevent cracking, another key is to allow adequate spacing among fruits as they grow — one of the hallmarks of training plants to grow up. Allow 24 to 30 inches (30–76 cm) between plants and pinch out excessive growth. Pinching extra flowers will also trick heavily bearing, determinate varieties into producing earlier, larger, and tastier fruit.

TRAINING TOMATOES TO GROW UP

There are nearly as many means of training tomatoes as there are varieties to choose from. Most methods require tying, because tomatoes do not climb; they support their weight by leaning against whatever is available and sprawling all over the ground if they have to. The type of support you'll need depends on the type and number of plants you grow as much as the size of your overall plot. With tomatoes, it's easy to get carried away.

Stakes

Perhaps the most traditional method is to drive a sturdy stake about 2 inches (5 cm) thick and 6 to 8 feet (2–2.5 m) long into the ground next to each seedling. This works as well for a long row of plants as it does for one precious vine. As the tomato vine grows, you will need to periodically tie it up and prune it to maintain its form. Pruning consists mainly of removing the suckers that grow in the joints between the main stem and a lateral branch. If left in place, these soon rival the trunk of the plant in size.

When choosing a tomato cage, remember to plan for the size of the fully grown plant, and make sure it is well anchored when you first set the seedlings in the ground.

Cages

Cages are the second most common way of containing rangy tomato plants and the most appropriate method for determinate varieties. You can purchase ready-made tomato cages or easily make your own by using tomato-cage wire, field fencing wire, or any suitable wire mesh with at least 6-inch (15 cm) openings in the mesh. Self-supporting, individual cages are a great choice for growing just a few plants.

More-attractive cages can be made from 1×2 lumber. Use 6-foot (2 m) wooden posts for the corners and nail or screw 1×2s to form ladders across the middle and top of the cage. Set the cages in place, then shove the posts into the soil to anchor the bottoms.

Arch Support

A wire-mesh arch is even easier than a cage. Cut a 6-foot (2 m) section of wire mesh, then bend it over the young tomato plant to form a tunnel. Draw the stems through the mesh as the plant grows, and allow them to amble down the sides. No tying or other training is necessary.

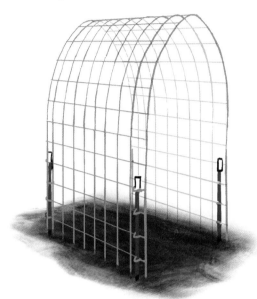

Use appropriate heavy-wire mesh to make an arch support; chicken wire is too flimsy.

Zigzag Posts

Here's another no-tie method that works great for multiple plants in one bed (see the illustration on page 29). Drive a stake or post into each corner of the bed and two more on opposite sides of the bed, spaced every 3 or 4 feet (1.5 m). As the plants grow, wrap twine around and between the posts, zigzagging across the middle of the bed and in between the plants. Add strands every 6 to 8 inches (15–20 cm) up the posts.

By the end of the season, you will have created a 4-foot-tall (1.5 m) or higher twine cage that supports the plants beautifully and is easy to reach through right up to harvest-time. The dense overlapping cuts weeds to almost nil and shades developing fruit from sunscald.

Twine Fence

Tomatoes can also be trained to a variety of fences. A good, simple fence consists of 4- to 6-foot (1.5–2 m) wooden stakes or posts driven between the plants with wire, twine, clothesline, or the like woven between the stakes and around the plants. The plants lean on the wires or twine and need no tying.

Arrange the rows to run north and south, and drive the stakes into the ground at a 20- to 30-degree angle toward the west. The weight of the fruits causes them to hang from the underside of the fence on the west side. Consequently, the morning sun hits the base and sides of the plant, and only the tops get full sunlight during the heat of the day. The fruit is protected from too much sun by the canopy of leaves. An A-frame trellis and a running tepee trellis work in much the same way.

Zigzag Fence

Another inventive fence is a zigzag fence (see the illustration on page 27). Cut 2½-foot (1 m) panels from 4-foot-high (1.5 m) wire mesh so that the open side is smooth and the other side has wire ends sticking out. Bend these ends over the smooth end of the next panel to form a hingelike connection.

Set up the fence over a row of tomato plants in a zigzag so each plant is supported on two sides. (Make sure to do this well before the plants grow too tall.) The open end makes a plant accessible for pruning, weeding, tying, and harvesting. Be sure to anchor the fence at the ends and the center with 6-foot (2 m) metal or wooden stakes that are driven 2 feet (61 cm) into the ground.

One of the best things about this fence is that after the harvest is over and the vines are cut away, it quickly and neatly folds for storage.

CHAPTER 8

CUCUMBERS

Why do we say "cool as a cucumber" when cucumbers adore warm, sunny summer days? Cool weather puts them in a slump: They will not grow, they will not set fruit, and they often succumb to disease. If you respect their sensitive nature, however, they are not that finicky to grow. Just give them good weather, plenty of water, and a stress-free life, and they will produce more crispy, green picklers and slicers than you will know what to do with!

VARIETIES

Cucumbers (*Cucumis sativus*) are generally divided into two types: picklers and slicers. (Some are touted as "dual-purpose," meaning they are good either pickled or fresh.) Excellent cultivars, many resistant to disease, are available in both categories. Plus, there are a few oddball, or novelty, varieties grown for their unusual looks as much as for eating quality. As with other vining crops, hybrids tend to grow shorter vines than open-pollinated varieties.

Pickling Cukes

Pickling varieties have flavorful, crunchy flesh and thin skin covered with small spines or bumps. They are also known for producing bumper crops of small fruit — from 2 to 6 inches (15 cm) long.

There's nothing like a few jars of your own homemade pickles to brighten up the winter months.

NATIONAL PICKLING (F1 hybrid, 50–55 days, MO) is an old favorite for good reasons. It starts early and produces prolifically throughout the season. Best pickled while fruit is still small and blocky, with tender skin and crisp flesh, it is also popular as a slicer for its mild flavor when grown to full size. Vines are vigorous and disease resistant.

CALYPSO (hybrid, 50 days, GY) is another heavily productive, disease-resistant variety, also valued as a dual-purpose cuke. It has long, straggling vines.

ROYAL (F1 hybrid, 60 days, GY) is a favorite pickler, with high yields that keep coming all season. It grows well in most regions.

WISCONSIN SMR (OP, 55–58 days, MO) is considered the top open-pollinated cucumber for dill pickles, producing heavy yields of small, exceptionally crisp, sweet fruit. The vines can reach 8 feet (2.5 m) long, do well in the North, and are resistant to scab and cucumber mosaic virus.

WHEN IS A GHERKIN NOT A CUCUMBER?

Always, actually. Gherkins are extra-small, extra-spiny varieties of a different species from regular cucumbers. If you're a gherkin fan, try **Mexican sour gerkin** (*Melothria scabra*) (OP, 50 days). These tiny, 2-inch (5 cm), watermelon look-alikes flood the plant's rambunctious vines, then fall off when ripe. They make wonderful sweet pickles. Eaten fresh, they have a sweet cucumber flavor with a sour aftertaste.

Slicing Cukes

Slicing cucumbers are eaten fresh and prized for their mild flavor in sandwiches and salads. They generally produce fruits 8 inches (20 cm) to over a foot (30 cm) long that may curl or twist unless trained up a trellis or other vertical support. There are several types (see also Novelty Cucumbers, on page 74) and scores of varieties.

One of the most popular types of slicing cucumber is the burpless variety (see Pardon Me: The Story behind Burpless Cukes, on page 75). There are so many varieties that the following sampling barely scratches the surface.

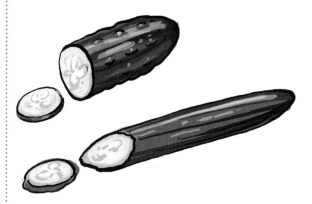

BURPLESS (hybrid, 62 days) was the original burpless variety. Its vigorous climbing vines produce sweet, long, mild-tasting, Oriental-type fruit. (See Orient Express, page 74.)

SWEET SUCCESS (hybrid, PAT, 54–58 days, 1983 AAS) produces seedless, 12-inch (30 cm) cukes that are sweet, crisp, and burpless. Vines grow to 6 feet (2 m) long and are resistant to cucumber mosaic virus, scab, and target leaf spot. If grown in a greenhouse or otherwise not allowed to pollinate, fruit will be seedless.

DIVA (hybrid, GY, 58 days, 2002 AAS) offers dark green cucumbers, which at their peak of 6 to 8 inches (15–20 cm) long are crisp, sweet, and burpless. Vines grow to 6 feet (2 m) and are strongly resistant to powdery mildew, scab, downy mildew, and cucumber mosaic virus.

STRAIGHT 8 (OP, 58–65 days, AAS, MO) is another long-time favorite with its excellent flavor and consistently dark green, 8-inch-long (20 cm) fruit. Vines are vigorous and produce continuously. A newer version, **STRAIGHT 9**, is similar, with improved disease resistance.

Novelty Cucumbers

Novelty cucumbers can add an exotic gourmet touch to your table as well as the garden. Though most are best eaten fresh, some make excellent, if unusual-looking, picklers.

LEMON, also called **CRYSTAL APPLE** (OP, 65 days), produces oval, lemon-sized, pale yellow fruit with mild, white flesh. Vines grow to 7 feet (2.5 m) long and produce abundant yields. Harvest at 1½-half inches (4 cm) across for pickling and at about 2 inches (5 cm) for fresh eating. A lack of cucurbitacins ensures that they are never bitter.

PEARL (hybrid, 57 days, GY) is most noticed for its striking greenish white color, yet is superbly adaptable to different growing conditions. It has outstanding flavor and crispness, and is best when harvested at about 6 inches (15 cm) long.

ORIENT EXPRESS II (hybrid, 64 days, GY) is an Oriental-type cucumber, meaning it produces 10- to 14-inch-long (25–36 cm), slender, dark green, mild-flavored, tender-skinned, burpless fruit. This variety is especially disease resistant and productive, and has a longer than normal shelf life.

BIRGIT (hybrid, 64 days, GY) is a European type, with dark green, 14-inch-long (36 cm), narrow, burpless fruit with slightly ribbed skin.

ARMENIAN CUCUMBERS (*Cucumis melo* var. *flexuosus*), or Snake Cucumbers, technically aren't cucumbers at all, but rather a variety of melon. Some grow 2 to 3 feet (61–91 cm) long but are best harvested at 12 to 18 inches (30–46 cm) in length. Untrellised, they produce S-shaped fruit. Burpless and mild flavored, they have ribbed or ridged skin. Some varieties are striped dark and light green, others a ghostly pale green.

SITE AND SOIL REQUIREMENTS

Cucumbers like full sun and lots of it. It is also important not to plant them where previous cucumbers, or related plants such as squash, pumpkins, and melons, have grown within the last three years. Diseases common to all can hide out in the soil for at least a year.

Cucumbers flourish in soils high in organic matter and nutrients. They prefer a well-worked, slightly acid (pH 5.5 to 7), well-drained soil. The best way to provide all this pampering is to work in generous amounts of compost or well-rotted manure prior to planting.

PLANTING GUIDELINES

Cucumber vines may be either started indoors or directly seeded into the garden. Be forewarned, however: Cucumbers and their relatives do not like to be transplanted.

Once the soil is well warmed (70°F [21°C]), dig 2 inches (5 cm) of compost into the soil or add a weak, well-balanced fertilizer (5-10-5 or 10-10-10) to get them off to a climbing start. Mound the soil into a hill or plant in raised beds. The raised soil warms faster and drains well, which are two things cucumbers really appreciate.

To seed directly, sow seeds ½ to 1 inch (1.5–2.5 cm) deep, 4 to 6 inches (10–15 cm) apart. Lightly press down the soil and water it well. The seeds will germinate in 7 to 14 days. After three sets of true leaves have developed, cut out all but the best plants every 12 inches (30 cm) or so at the base of the supports.

To start cucumbers indoors, wait until three to four weeks before the last frost. If you start them any earlier, the plants will grow too large by transplant time. To minimize stress and get the best results, transplants should have no more than three sets of true leaves when they go in the ground. Although cucumbers resent any sort of disruption, especially transplanting, you can minimize the aggravation by using peat pots, disks, or other biodegradable containers.

Grow the seedlings on a sunny windowsill or under lights until they are ready to set out into the garden. Be sure to harden them off first (see Appendix 4), then set the plants, pots and all, into the ground so that the containers are well covered with soil. A transplant solution, such as a weak fish emulsion, will give the seedlings a boost. Water them in well, and keep the seedlings covered at first to protect them against any unanticipated drops in nighttime temperatures.

Shallow roots mean cucumbers are thirsty plants. A thorough watering once a week with adequate time for the soil to drain — not dry out — in between is ideal. Mulching them helps keep the soil from drying, as it shades and cools the roots and prevents weeds, all vastly appreciated by these voracious vines. Remember that cucumber roots feed near the soil surface, so avoid disrupting them

PARDON ME
The Story behind Burpless Cukes

No cucumbers burp, but compounds called **cucurbitacins** produced in the skin of the fruit can have an adverse effect on the digestive system of those who eat them. Cucurbitacins also taste bitter, ruining the best cucumber sandwich. Heat or drought stress on the plants increases the output of these unpleasant substances.

Due to genetic differences, one person in five can't taste cucurbitacins at all, which explains why some people think others are nuts when they complain about bitter-tasting cucumbers. But two in five people have an acute sensitivity to cucurbitacins, which makes it understandable if they think the rest of us are nuts for eating cucumbers at all.

The standard solution to the problem used to be simply peeling the offending skin. But people are not the only ones affected by cucurbitacins. Insect pests are attracted to the compounds and zero in on cucumber plants that produce them, either naturally or through stress. So when plant breeders developed "burpless" varieties, with little to no cucurbitacin in the skins, everyone was happy but the bugs.

by hand pulling or hoeing too deeply. As the vines begin to flower, apply a top dressing of organic fertilizer to give them a fruit-setting boost.

TRAINING CUCUMBERS TO GROW UP

Cucumbers really benefit from trellising. Even "dwarf" varieties produce superior fruit when levitated aboveground, whether climbing a support or cascading down the sides of a container or hanging basket. Most are extremely susceptible to diseases brought on by the high humidity and poor air circulation so typical of grounded vines. Misshapen fruit is also a

common product of grounded vines. Those same plants, however, will develop straight fruit when hanging from a support.

Related vine crops, such as squash and melons, do not cross with cucumbers.

Cucumbers climb by tightly coiling tendrils, whose slow-motion grasp is ever reaching upward. A soft tie here and there helps train them in the right place, especially on a vertical or angled trellis. Fence-type trellises with wire mesh for plant support work well for cucumbers.

A-frames, pipe, and wooden-lattice designs can also be used with good results. Some gardeners caution that wire or metal may overheat and burn the tendrils or leaves, but the leaves should shade the frame well enough to prevent this. Wire and pipe can be wrapped with florists' tape or cloth strips to prevent it from burning the vines.

The zigzag design of an A-frame trellis is very popular for cucumbers. It is easily relocated year after year to facilitate crop rotation, and cucumbers find the sloping sides easy to scale (see page 27).

Without proper support, cucumber vines will sprawl all over the ground, making it hard to find the fruit, let alone pick it.

THE SECRET LIFE OF CUCUMBERS

If you think your sex life is complicated, be grateful you're not a cucumber.

Some cucumber plants are **gynoecious** (GY), which means they produce only female (fruiting) flowers. Some are **monoecious** (MO), producing both male and female flowers on the same plant. Most readily available varieties fall into one or the other of these categories.

You can identify which flowers are male and which are female by looking for a tiny bulge behind the blossom that looks like a miniature cucumber; only female flowers have it. Gynoecious varieties bear heavier yields than monoecious types, provided they are pollinated by a male flower from a separate plant.

Nurseries and seed sellers include male-flowering pollinators with gynoecious plants or seeds to ensure fruit set. (Male seeds are often dyed for easy identification.)

A Helping Hand

In plants that produce both male and female flowers, often the first blooms to appear are the fruitless males, which soon drop off the vine. Remember, only female flowers set fruit. First, however, they must receive pollen from male flowers, a process that depends on insects — primarily bees.

If your vines are not fruiting, you can give nature a hand by doing the job yourself. Pluck the petals from a male flower and rub the pollen-covered anthers gently around the inside of a female blossom. The pollen will adhere to the sticky stigma, work its way to the blossom's ovaries, and soon a cucumber is born!

Different cucumber varieties can cross-pollinate, but this affects only the next generation of seeds, not the current season's fruit harvest. The exception is parthenogenic cukes, those that set fruit without pollination. These are often grown in a greenhouse or under covers right up until harvest to prevent accidental/unwanted pollination.

Unpollinated, they produce seedless cucumbers or, at most, with some tiny vestiges of seeds. If pollinated, the fruit is still fine, but will contain sterile or, at best, unproductive seeds, like other cucumbers.

CHAPTER 9

SQUASH
AND
GOURDS

Many gardeners draw the line right here. For those with limited space, the idea of these massive trailing vines is disheartening if not downright terrifying. But once you know how to tame these beasts, the rewards are well worth the effort.

Squash and gourds (*Cucurbita pepo, C. moschata*, and *C. maxima*) are closely related to cucumbers. They are available in many varieties of healthful, tasty fruits and are so prolific and easy to grow that no garden should be deprived of them. If space has been your only objection to the cornucopia of their various delights, or if plant diseases or poorly developed fruit have soured you on squash, cheer up!

By training them to grow up, you can grow beautiful, bountiful squash and gourds anywhere you have a few inches of ground space and at least six hours of direct sunlight.

VARIETIES

Squash and gourds offer some of the largest selections of plant varieties in the garden. They can be little or big, in colors that include white, yellow, orange, and green with stripes and patterns galore. There are fancy scallops, bells, clubs, straight and crooked necks, and rounded shapes from the size of tennis balls to beach ball–size.

Squash are divided into summer squash and winter squash, and then again into many subtypes. Most gardeners are familiar with summer squash (usually zucchini) that grow as squatty, bush-type plants, but true vining varieties are available as well. They are harvested throughout the season while still immature.

Winter varieties typically grow on endless meandering vines and are harvested just once at the end of the season. Gourds, too, offer an astonishing array of varieties, some of which are edible (at least when immature) and most of which are decorative or functional.

Summer Squash Vines

Vining summer squash varieties are less common than their compact cousins, but when space is at a premium, they can turn a patch of ground space along a fence or wall into a zucchini lover's dream. Most summer squash varieties, such as pattypan, yellow crookneck, zucchini, and Italian squash, are predominantly sold as bush types, though vining examples are available.

A couple of summer squash vines can produce an enormous crop, giving rise to many jokes about people sneaking piles of zucchini onto their neighbors' porches or leaving them in unlocked cars.

Trailing zucchini-type squash is easier to find online or in seed catalogs if you look for words like *courgette* or *marrow*. Courgettes are picked at about 4 inches (10 cm) long; marrows at about 8 to 10 inches (20–25 cm) long. Varieties are *Cucurbita pepo* unless otherwise noted.

....

Squash, pumpkins, gourds, cucumbers, and melons are called cucurbits.

....

ZUCCHETTA RAMPICANTE-TROMBONCINO (OP, 60 days) is an Italian variety known for its enthusiastic trailing growth; it needs strong support. Fruit is light yellowish green and mild-flavored. They are delicious when harvested at about 10 inches (25 cm) long, but can grow to giant twisted monsters if left on the vine.

TABLE DAINTY (OP, 110 days) is a green and yellow striped, English trailing marrow that can be harvested young and used like zucchini or allowed to mature to stuffing size.

LONG GREEN TRAILING or **TRAILING GREEN MARROW** (OP, 70 days) can grow very large, so keep it picked back to ensure a steady (edible!) crop.

BLACK FOREST F1 (hybrid, 91–95 days) produces an abundance of dark green, cylindrical, 6-inch (15 cm) courgette fruits, just like the bush-type zucchini most of us are used to.

GEM SQUASH, also known as **LITTLE GEM** or **GEM STORE** (OP, 80 days), forms black/green-skinned, orange-fleshed, perfectly round balls on ranging vines. Its fruit is most tender at golf ball size. Drought-tolerant, it develops a tough shell when mature.

TATUME (OP, 45–61 days) is native to Mexico and will produce mild-flavored, greenish to yellow, 5- to 7-inch (13 to 18 cm) rounded fruit even under near drought conditions.

TROMBONCINO (OP, 80 days) produces very long (up to 3 feet [1 m]!), narrow, firm, flavorful, pale green Italian summer squash with seeds limited to one small cavity at the very end.

Winter Squash

Winter squash are harvested at maturity after the skin has hardened into a protective rind. They are so named because, when cured properly, they should store through the winter (ideally at 45–55°F [7 to 13°C]). There are several types, such as acorn, butternut, hubbard, spaghetti squash, and a few that defy neat categorization. Pumpkins are a type of winter squash (see page 82).

Acorn Squash

Acorn squash (*C. pepo*) is so-named because of its shape. It has a nutlike flavor, golden to orange flesh, and a seed well at the center of the fruit.

TABLE QUEEN (OP, 85 days) is a sweet, delicately flavored, deeply ribbed variety that tends toward long vines yielding four or five squash each.

MESA QUEEN (F1, hybrid, 70 days) is much like its counterpart above, except that the vines are a bit shorter and bear about seven fruits apiece.

THELMA SANDERS' SWEET POTATO (OP, 85–95 days) produces wonderfully flavored, excellently textured, thick-fleshed, pale gold fruit up to 8 inches (20 cm) long.

Butternut Squash

Butternut squash (*C. moschata*) produces distinctive bell-shaped fruits that are exceptional winter keepers. Fruits can be heavy, so plan on using slings or other supports.

WALTHAM BUTTERNUT (OP, 100 days, AAS) is the gold standard, with 8- to 10-foot-long (2.5–3 m) vines bearing four or five large squash each. Flesh is yellow-orange with a rich, nutty flavor and dry texture.

NOT YOUR GRANDMA'S SQUASH

Here are a couple of more unusual varieties that are worth a try.

DELICATA (OP, 97 days) puts out 6- to 8-inch-long (15–20 cm) fruit just bursting with sweet potato flavor. Each vine offers six or seven cream- and dark-green–striped fruit.

PINK BANANA (OP, 100 days) sounds funny and sure looks odd with its pinkish, cylindrical fruit growing up to 30 inches (76 cm) long, but it is *so* sweet! The yellow-orange flesh is thick and firm, never stringy, and great for all-around cooking and baking.

GOING OUT OF YOUR GOURD

True gourds (*Lagenaria siceraria*) were a symbol in early Chinese mythology for the concept of "chaosmos" — the order within chaos. And given the crazy shapes, sizes, and colors they encompass, it's a fitting tribute.

Some are edible, especially when small, but most often it is their diverse usefulness that lands them a spot in the garden. Most grow quickly in warm climates, adding "camouflage for an ugly wall or fence" to their résumés. The following is just a small sampling of the varieties available.

The Tough Guys

True gourds produce smallish white flowers that develop into greenish fruits that mature in shades of tan or brown. They develop hard shells, some as dense and tough as wood. They are best known as crafting gourds. Some varieties grow very large: up to 30 inches (76 cm) long and 50 pounds (22.5 kg)! Here are a few more suitable to growing up.

BIRDHOUSE (OP, 120 days) is so called because it is most often grown to make birdhouses, especially for purple martins. Finished gourds are 5 by 10 inches (13×25 cm) or larger.

BOTTLE (OP, 90 to 120 days), a form of calabash gourd also called **Birdhouse,** is a manic climber with a great deal of variety within the subtype. Easy to grow, it is almost pest- and disease-free. The immature fruit can be cooked and eaten.

LONG-HANDLED DIPPER (OP, 125 days) grows a long "handle" ending in a 4-inch (10 cm) ovoid globe. The perfect shape and size for dipping gives this variety its name and practical history. Trained to grow up, the handle will develop long and straight as the fruit hangs down; allowed to sprawl, it will twist and curl.

On the Softer Side

Soft-shelled gourds are actually varieties of *C. pepo.* They produce large, edible yellow flowers that grow into fruits in a wild array of shapes and colors. Great for decorations, they make the Thanksgiving table centerpiece complete. They are not recommended for crafts, as the shells are too soft.

KOSHARE YELLOW (OP, 95–100 days) produces green-and-yellow-banded fruit whose color patterns are determined by the temperature during flower development. They hold their bright colors well over a long time and make exceptional decorations.

AUTUMN WINGS (OP, 100 days) are spoon-shaped little gourds, no more than 3½ inches (9 cm) in length, with top-to-bottom flares that look like, well, wings. They brightly display fall colors of white, yellow, gold, orange, russet, and deep green.

GOBLIN EGGS (OP, 85 days), in keeping with the holiday theme, are egg-sized, egg-shaped gourds borne generously on productive plants. Colors erupt in the same palette as above with solids, patchwork patterns, and stripes.

EARLY BUTTERNUT (hybrid, 85 days) has deep red-orange flesh that is sweet and delicately flavored. Fruit averages 2 pounds (1 kg) each, four or five per vine.

Hubbard Squash

Hubbard squash (*C. maxima*) might be the crop that separates the garden-variety gardeners from the rising stars. Hefty vines produce massive fruits with flavor so rich, sweet, and tender that they are worth all the extra tying and support they require.

SUGAR HUBBARD (OP, 110 days) produces four or five sweet, moist, 15-pound (6 kg) squash on 10-foot-long (3 m) vines. Renowned keepers, they can store for up to a year.

SWEET MEAT (OP, 115 days) produces light gray, round squash with the richest, sweetest flavor imaginable. The vines grow to 10 feet (3 m) long; fruits to 15 pounds (6 kg). It's an excellent keeper.

Spaghetti Squash

Spaghetti squash are so called because the fibrous flesh, baked and scooped out, can pass for a low-starch pasta any day. Great with spaghetti sauce!

SPAGHETTI (OP, 100 days) produces 8-inch (20 cm), tannish yellow fruit on 5- to 6-foot (1.5–2 m) -long vines.

SMALL WONDER (hybrid, 80 days) answers the call for a single-serving spaghetti squash with 3-pound (1.5 kg), 5- to 6-inch (12–15 cm), golden-colored squash with a creamy yellow interior. A great keeper.

Pumpkins

The pumpkin (*C. pepo*) is one of the most recognizable fruits on the planet. International symbol of the harvest and a familiar North

All but the largest pumpkins can be successfully trained upward rather than be allowed to take over the garden.

American grinning (or grimacing!) ambassador of goblin goodwill, a pumpkin is loved by all.

Cooking pumpkins (listed below) tend to be smaller at maturity and easier to support on a trellis, and have thicker, less stringy flesh than those grown for carving. Many of both types have edible seeds. A few are good both for eating and as holiday ornaments.

JACK-BE-LITTLE (OP, 85–100 days) grows to only 3 inches (8 cm) across with as few as six and as many as a dozen fruits on short (for a pumpkin), 5-foot vines. Best loved as decorations, they can be baked for a small treat.

AUTUMN GOLD (F1 hybrid, 90 days, AAS) forms perfect globes, up to 10 pounds (4.5 kg) each, with smooth skin and deep, rich, autumn orange color. Great for baking and carving.

TRIPLE TREAT (hybrid, 110 days) is an excellent all-purpose pumpkin with sweet and tasty flesh. Bake it into pies, toast the seeds, or carve the shell for Halloween. Vines are 10 to 12 feet (3–3.5 m) long.

SMALL SUGAR (OP, 110 days) is *the* pie pumpkin and is treasured for its fine flavor and smooth texture. Vines produce four to six 7-inch (18 cm) pumpkins each.

EARLY SWEET SUGAR PIE (hybrid, 90 days) is considered among the very best for pies, with its fine orange flesh and rich pumpkiny flavor. Fruits weigh in at 6 to 7 pounds (2.5–3 kg).

FORTUNA WHITE (*C. mixta*, OP, 85 days) is one to try if you are ready for something really different. Sweet, creamy yellow flesh in a stark white, bell-shaped, 10-pound (4.5 kg) package makes this a delightful Pennsylvania heirloom.

SITE AND SOIL REQUIREMENTS

Like the majority of other vine crops, squash and gourds grow best in full sun and warm temperatures. They demand good drainage and plenty of water. Slightly acidic (6 to 6.5 pH) soil, rich in humus, will help to satisfy these requirements; work in compost or rotted manure to keep organic matter and nutrient levels high.

Colloidal or rock phosphate can be added to boost phosphorus levels, and greensand or wood ashes can be supplied to raise the level of potash, if needed.

PLANTING GUIDELINES

Like all cucurbits, squash and gourds are extremely frost sensitive and fussy about transplanting, which can make it frustrating to get them in the ground early enough. For many types of winter squash and most gourds, which can take up to 120 days to mature, an early start is absolutely essential for anyone gardening in all but the most temperate zones (8 and warmer).

Help winter squash and gourds to mature by picking off any flowers that form after midsummer, since they will not have a chance to mature and will only drain the plant's energy if left. Summer squash, however, can produce all season.

There are two ways to cater to their needs. If your frost-free days are only a few weeks short of the time needed to grow a particular variety to maturity, start the seeds indoors in 4-inch (10 cm) peat pots four to six weeks before the last frost. Once the garden soil is

ROCK-A-BYE PUMPKIN

For very large fruit, say more than 30 pounds (13.5 kg), slings often don't help much because the weight tears them or pulls down the vine support. It's easy to underestimate just how heavy a vine loaded with pumpkins or large squashes can become!

The vines can still be trellised to good advantage, though, by building in platforms to hold those giant fruits. These can be engineered into a sturdy trellis design or improvised from an overturned bucket, step ladder, or bales of straw, depending on how high up the vine the fruit grows.

See pages 17 and 96 for more on using slings to support large fruit.

well warmed, transplant the seedlings to the garden in the pots, and make sure that the tops of the peat pots are well covered with soil.

If, however, your garden falls far short of the warm season needed for these plants, start indoors as many weeks in advance of the last frost date as necessary. Figure out this date by counting the weeks backwards from your average first frost date in the fall. The pot must be large enough, gallon size (3.5 L) or better, for the plants to get a good start without becoming in any way rootbound.

A large pot also helps to ensure as little root disturbance as possible at transplant time. Biodegradable pots (made from peat, pressed manure, or even old newspaper) help minimize root disturbance even further. Like the 4-inch (10 cm) pots, the entire planter goes into the ground at transplant time.

A half-an-A-frame design works well to support sprawling squash vines while providing easy access for harvesting.

Follow the general rules of hardening the seedlings off, transplanting them in the evening or on an overcast day to diminish the shock and then protecting them at night until all danger of frost is past.

Like their relatives, squash and gourds like the superior drainage and the warmer soil provided by raised beds or hill planting. Leave about 2 feet (61 cm) between plants in raised beds, or space hills so that the centers are about 4 feet (121 cm) apart. (Untrellised plants require much more space between them because the vines take up so much room.) Up to four transplants can go into each hill, or plant eight seeds an inch (2.5 cm) deep and snip out all but the best three or four as they grow.

> One inventive gardener enlisted three old stepladders to stand guard over his squash hills, with very satisfactory results.

Mound the soil into hills about 18 inches (46 cm) across and 10 inches (25 cm) high, then form a depression in the center. The depression holds water and allows it to slowly drain to the plant roots rather than run off the sides of the hill. Seeds will not germinate in soil temperatures lower than 60°F (16°C), so make sure the ground is warm before you plant.

TRAINING SQUASH TO GROW UP

The best candidates for growing up are lightweight, small-fruited squash and gourds, though all but the heaviest can be trellised, given a sturdy enough frame and strong enough materials. Fruits from one to a few

Traditionally used for beans, a well-grounded tepee of sturdy poles works equally well for a couple of squash plants, especially ones that produce smaller fruit.

individual fruits. Slings, however, are cheap insurance when it comes to a prize pumpkin or squash, so you may want to include them just to be safe (see pages 17 and 96).

Several forms of trellises are suitable for squash or gourds. Tailor the design to fit your planting area and the type of fruit to be supported. Tepees of heavy poles, 8 feet (2.5 m) long and at least 2 inches (5 cm) thick, make a practical, sturdy, and inexpensive framework. Squash vines really appreciate the extra horizontal support that can be provided by weaving rope around and through the tepee legs.

If planting in individual hills, a tepee trellis is perfect because it can be set up directly over the mound to provide a leg to support each plant. Other designs that have proved successful with squash and gourds are the fence types and A-frames (see pages 25–28). A single cattle panel, held in place at an angle to form a lean-to, should support a dozen vines.

You will need to have a few strips of cloth or recycled plastic grocery bags to tie the vines in place as they grow. Different varieties have different growth habits, but squash and gourds typically grow more perfectly shaped, cleaner, evenly colored fruit when the vines are trained up a support and the fruit hangs down freely.

pounds (0.5–2 kg) will need no additional support aside from tying the vines in place.

As the fruit gradually increases in size and weight, the vines grow ever stronger in proportion to the increasing burden. Some gardeners grow 10- to 15-pounders (4.5–7 kg fruit) without resorting to slings to support

CHAPTER 10

MELONS

Of the truly rare and satisfying pleasures in life, sampling a freshly picked, vine-ripened melon from your own garden ranks among the most elusive. These temperamental treats are often bypassed by gardeners, especially those in the North. But those undistinguished orbs available in supermarkets are a far cry from what the resourceful gardener can produce at home.

Due to the demands of the market, mass-produced melons must be picked according to a schedule dictated more by shipment and sales agendas than by ripeness. Meanwhile, the home gardener can take a daily stroll, inspecting each fruit for the one that is closest to ripe perfection to enjoy with lunch.

The reason for the immense difference in the flavor of homegrown versus supermarket melons is that once plucked from the vine, the sugars in melons do not continue to ripen. What you pick is what you get. Wouldn't you rather pick a scrumptious melon from your own backyard than a green gamble from the produce aisle?

VARIETIES

Another sad fact of market melons is the lack of variety. Although the selection available commercially is expanding, many more varieties are available for home growing.

There are two primary types of melons: the wide-ranging species *Cucumis melo*, which has seedless flesh and a seed cavity at the center of the fruit, and *Citrullus lanatus*, or watermelon, with seeds distributed throughout the flesh. *C. melo* is divided into several groups, only two of which (plus an odd stray or two) we'll tackle here.

Melons of the Cantalupensis group (which comprise Reticulatus or "netted skins") have aromatic flesh (which is why they're called muskmelons) in colors such as salmon, orange, and even green. This group includes true cantaloupes, which have no netting and North American cantaloupes, which have a netted rind.

The Inodorous group represents nonaromatic, non-netted melons with green or white or, rarely, orange flesh. Toss in a third, catch-all category of "exotic" or "specialty melons," and you begin to see the wide range of sweet tastes just waiting for you to discover them. The following list is by no means exhaustive, but it presents some of the better candidates for growing vertically.

The first cantaloupe cultivar was named for Cantalupo, the town of its origin near Rome.

True Cantaloupes

True cantaloupes (*Cucumis melo* group Cantaloupensis), also called European cantaloupes, are best represented in American home gardens by the Charentais and Cavaillon types. Modern varieties have lengthwise grooves, called sutures, but no netting. Their high sugar content and thin skin do not hold up to shipping, which destines them to the home garden and thus relative obscurity, except for the hardy of hoe and the adventurous of vine.

CHARENTAIS, generic named (OP, 90 days), has a thin, smooth skin with light green stripes that matures to a creamy yellow. The orange flesh is fine-textured, delightfully scented, and very sweet.

> True cantaloupes are considered by (French) connoisseurs to be the very best melons on the planet.

TROCADERO (hybrid, 75 days) grows vigorous vines that produce 2-pound, grayish to creamy yellow, perfumed fruit with a gourmet taste. Unlike other Charentais varieties, Trocadero fruit slip from the stem when ripe. Resistant to powdery mildew and fusarium wilt.

FRENCH ORANGE (F1 hybrid, 75 days) is a cross between Charentais and *C. melo reticulate* cultivar. Heavenly flavored, crack-resistant round fruits are netted and have deep orange, intensely aromatic flesh.

SAVOR (hybrid, 85 days), with unsurpassed eating quality, is billed as the sweetest of the French melons. It is a prolific producer that is resistant to fusarium wilt and powdery mildew.

North American Cantaloupes

North American cantaloupes (*Cucumis melo*, group Cantalupensis, subgroup Reticulatus) are a type of muskmelon. Cantaloupe skins turn from green to cream colored and form a raised, tan netting on the rind as the fruit ripens. When ripe, the flesh may be bright orange, golden, salmon, or even green.

AMBROSIA (F1 hybrid, 83–86 days), with its familiar cantaloupe look, flavor, and aroma, is a sweet, juicy favorite. Fruit is medium

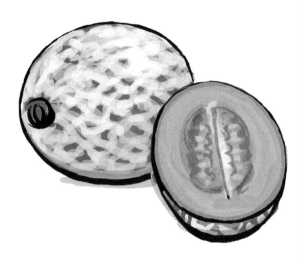

Homegrown melons are more likely to be consistently sweet and juicy than the ones found in supermarket bins.

sized (to 5 pounds [2 kg]) and heavily netted with salmon-colored flesh. Vines are resistant to powdery mildew.

BURPEE HYBRID (hybrid, 82 days) produces 3- to 4½-pound (2 kg), 6- to 7-inch (15–18 cm), deeply ribbed, heavily netted, flavorful fruit. The thick flesh is orange, firm, and juicy, surrounding a small seed cavity. Resistant to powdery mildew.

HALE'S BEST (OP, 86 days) is an old-time favorite beloved for its sweet taste. Fruit grows to 5 or 6 pounds (2–2.5 kg), with thick flesh and a small seed cavity.

HONEY ROCK (OP, 83 days, 1933 AAS) boasts thick, sweet, firm, salmon-orange-colored flesh on vines that produce five to seven fruits each.

A Few Oddballs

Other muskmelons (for lack of a more imaginative category) offer a range of interesting fruits that just don't fit the cantaloupe category.

JENNY LIND (OP, 70–85 days) is an old heirloom that looks quirky with its small (1- to 2-pound [0.5–1 kg]), dark green, turban-shaped fruit, but its lime green flesh is sweet. Vines grow to 5 feet (1.5 m) long, are disease resistant, and become prolific producers.

EDEN GEM, also known as Rocky Ford (OP, 65–80 days), produces luscious, heavily netted and ribbed, soft-ball-sized fruit (about a pound [0.5 kg] each) on reliable vines. Flavor is spicy/sweet.

ISRAELI or **OGEN,** sold generically and as named varieties (OP and hybrid varieties, 85 days), has a history that's a jealously guarded secret. It was developed in a kibbutz in Israel in the 1960s and not released for decades — and for good reason. Melons are 3 to 5 pounds (1.5–2 kg), changing

NOT WHAT YOU THINK

Most of what are commonly referred to as cantaloupes in North America aren't true cantaloupes at all but an entirely different subgroup of *C. melo.* True cantaloupes, *C. melo cantaloupensis,* look very different from what North Americans think of as cantaloupes; the surface is not netted, but instead deeply grooved. They are grown primarily in Europe.

To make matters even more confusing, muskmelons, which to North Americans are synonymous with cantaloupes, encompass far more than just the single type we identify as cantaloupes. Muskmelons — including but not limited to *Cucumis melo* group Cantaloupensis subgroup Reticulatus, the netted types of melons — are named for their heady aroma.

from light green to lightly netted gold at maturity, exceptionally flavored, rich, and aromatic. Productive plants are recommended for northern gardens. Tough competition to beat!

PERSIAN MELONS, sold generically and as named varieties (OP and hybrid varieties, 90–115 days), grow 5- or 6-pound (2.5–3 kg), round or football-shaped fruit with faint netting over dark green skin. The flesh is pinkish orange, milder, and firmer than that of muskmelons. They do not slip at maturity but remain hanging on the vine (provided with adequate support) when ripe.

Winter Melons

Winter melons (*Cucumis melo* group Inodorus) are melons that mature late and keep well (into the winter). Among them are honeydews, casabas, crenshaws, Christmas, and canary melons.

Honeydews

Honeydews were introduced to Americans by the French in 1911 as a single variety called White Antibes. Now there are dozens of varieties and hybrids. They typically have pale green to creamy white skin that can be smooth, faintly downy, or very finely netted, and firm, sweet, light green flesh. Some varieties offer amber-colored flesh and designer flavors such as pear, apple, and pineapple. Smaller varieties typically do best on trellises.

EARLIDEW (F1 hybrid, 80 days) is the best bet for cooler climates. Fruits are 5 to 6 inches (15 cm) in diameter and weigh 2 to 3 pounds (1–1.5 kg). The skin turns to near white at maturity. Resistant to fusarium wilt.

ORANGE FLESH (hybrid, 105 days) produces sweet, sweet, sweet, 3-pound (1.5 kg) fruit with thick, pale orange, juicy flesh.

Honeydew

Crenshaw

Casaba

These are just a few of the many types of winter melons available to the home gardener.

ANANAS D'AMERIQUE À CHAIR VERTE (OP, 90 days) is an old variety reportedly grown by Thomas Jefferson at Monticello in 1794. Long, vigorous, productive vines produce 5-pound (2 kg) fruit with pale green flesh that is firm, superbly sweet, and highly scented.

AM-04-16 (hybrid, 65–75 days) is a custom mini-version of the Ananas-type melon with fruits averaging about 1 to 1½ pounds (0.5 to 0.75 kg) apiece. Great-tasting, golden-skinned fruits have near-white flesh. Plants are resistant to fusarium wilt (races 0, 1, and 2) and powdery mildew (race 1).

> Don't plant melons where they or any other members of the cucurbit family have grown within the last three years to avoid soilborne pests or diseases.

Casabas

Casabas are rounded melons that are flat at the flower end and come to a point at the stem end. In late summer, the wrinkled skin ripens to a golden yellow and the lightly sweet, juicy flesh matures to a creamy white. Fruit matures at 4 to 8 pounds (2–3.5 kg). Historically, they are most appreciated for their long shelf life.

SUNGOLD MELON (hybrid, 95 to 105 days) is a short-season casaba that can be grown in the North. Fruits weigh 3 to 5 pounds (1.5–2 kg) each.

GOLDEN BEAUTY (OP, 100 days) is best adapted to hot, dry climates. Fruit grows up to 6 inches (15 cm) with a tough, wrinkly rind. The interior is white, fragrant, and spicy.

Crenshaws

Crenshaws (also spelled Cranshaws) are a cross between casaba and Persian melons. Slightly oblong fruit are pointed at the stem end and have slightly wrinkled, yellow or white skin at maturity (most people prefer the yellow). Standard varieties can grow up to 14 pounds (6 kg). The thick, peach- or salmon-colored flesh is uniquely flavored, and the ripe fruit is exceptionally fragrant.

LILLY (hybrid, 80 days) has a rich, sweet flavor in a smaller-than-average (6- to 8-pound [3 to 3.5 kg]) Crenshaw. Light orange flesh is creamy textured and juicy with a distinctive, spicy/sweet taste. The skin is pale yellow when ripe. Resistant to powdery mildew (races 1 and 2), melon mosaic virus, and potato mosaic virus.

SWEET FRECKLES (hybrid, 100 days) is an early Crenshaw about half the size of standard varieties. Fruits are speckled like an ocelot with dark green freckles that lighten as the fruit ripens. Flesh is light orange, sweet, and vaguely rose-scented.

Christmas Melons

Christmas or Santa Claus melons are football-shaped fruit that average from 5 to 8 pounds (2–3.5 kg). Named for their excellent storage properties, they will keep their eating quality until Christmas if harvested late and stored in a cool place.

LAMBKIN (hybrid, 65–75 days, 2008 AAS) weighs in at only 2 to 4 pounds (1–2 kg), making it a great prospect for vertical training. Vines produce four or five melons each of yellow and green mottled fruit with a thin rind and sweet, luscious flesh.

ST. NICK (hybrid, 84 days) grows to 5 or 6 pounds (2.5–3 kg) with a dark green, striated skin covering pale, cream-colored, sweet, juicy, light-flavored flesh.

Canary Melons

Canary melons are bright yellow, smooth, oval melons named for their color. Unlike the birds, however, most varieties tend to grow quite large, in excess of 5 pounds (2.5 kg) and up to 9 inches (23 cm) long. When ripe, they have a succulent, delicate flavor.

AMY (hybrid, 70–80 days, 2004 AAS) is just right for training up a support. Vines are long (6 feet [2 m]), and fruit are small (2 to 3 pounds [1–1.5 kg]) and deep golden when ripe, with a mild-tasting, white flesh.

OUT OF THE ORDINARY

"**E**xotic melons" covers a wide category of melons from around the world that can best be described as "other." Some are not even true melons at all; others are subgroups of the by now familiar *C. melo* species. So while the pickin's are anything but slim, consider this small list a good start. Check gardening catalogs for other ideas.

KIWANO (OP, 120 days) is a New Zealand import that grows prickly, ovoid fruit with a seedy, gelatinous center, the taste of which has been compared to a combination of pomegranate and citrus, or of banana and lime. Also known as Hedgehog Gourd, Jelly Melon, and African Horned Cucumber.

PIEL DE SAPO sold generically and as named varieties (OP, 90–110 days), means "toad skin" in Spanish. Melons are round to oblong with thick, ribbed, mottled, green skin and sweet, yellow to pale green flesh. Long vines (8 to 10 feet [2.5–3 m]) bear fruit up to 5 pounds (2 kg) each. It's a good keeper.

MANGO MELON (OP, 80–90 days) is reputed to be a Native American heirloom. It is easy to grow and very productive. The fruit is similar in size, shape, and color to oranges, but the unscented flesh is stark white with the texture of a mango. It tastes best when cooked. Vigorously spreading vines make this variety a great vertical choice.

TIGGER (OP, 85 days) is an Armenian immigrant with brilliant yellow-and-red-striped, 1-pound (0.5 kg) melons with semisweet, white flesh and astounding fragrance. This variety is similar to Queen Anne's Pocket — a tiny melon so fragrant that Victorian ladies would keep one in a pocket as perfume — but with better eating quality.

RAMPICANTE ZUCCHERINO (OP, 60–70 days from transplant; 80–90 days from direct seed) is an Italian heirloom whose name means "climbing sugar." Mature fruits are 2 to 2½ pounds (1 kg) and golden colored with sweet, orange flesh. A good climber.

NOIR DES CARMES (OP, 75 days) is a French import that is easy to grow. Black-skinned, immature fruit ripens to green-mottled orange. It is sweet, fragrant, and very productive.

PETIT GRIS DE RENNES (OP, 80–85 days) has survived the test of 400 years. First documented in the garden of the bishop of Rennes, France, it is still a fantastic melon for the home garden. Fruits are 2 to 3 pounds (1–1.5 kg), round, and smooth with wide ribs. Flesh is orange and sweet. Not a good keeper.

No longer restricted to the traditional and familiar red with black seeds, watermelons now come in several colors and in sizes to suit every garden.

Watermelons

Watermelons are the granddaddies of all home-grown melons, in more ways than one. Not only do they produce the biggest fruit on the longest vines, but they are also the oldest. The first watermelon crop on record was over 5,000 years ago in Egypt, where they were placed in the tombs of kings and pictured in hieroglyphics. And kids of all ages will tell you they are the sweetest and juiciest melon.

Today there are many choices for gardeners who want to grow their own watermelons. Sizes range from little 1- to 7-pounders (0.5–3 kg) up to enormous 100- to 200-pound (45–91 kg) zeppelins. (Giant Cobb Gem and Carolina Cross are examples of the latter. If you manage to grow one of these big boys on a trellis, send me a photo!) The vines are weaker than on many other trailing fruit and are not designed to hold up heavy melons, so even the smaller varieties need support.

If, like me, you remember being banned to the outdoors to enjoy big hunks of that sweet, red flesh — and dealing with all of those seeds by spitting for distance — there are a few surprises waiting for you in the watermelon patch. In addition to that beloved traditional type, yellow-fleshed varieties are now staples, as are ones with odd colors and flavors; personal, mini, or "icebox" types (the easiest to trellis); and, of course, many seedless varieties. Emily Post would be pleased.

Red Flesh

In spite of the variety of varieties available, red-fleshed watermelons are still favored by most sticky-chinned connoisseurs as the sweetest and tastiest. Here are a few petite favorites for growing up.

LITTLE BABY FLOWER (F1 hybrid, 70 days) offers 5½-inch (14 cm) round, 2- to 4-pound (1–2 kg) fruit with bright light and dark green stripes outside and deep dark pink flesh on the inside. Flesh is crisp and sweet. Plants average three to five fruits per vine.

Melons cross-pollinate readily, but the results affect only the seeds, not the current season's fruit.

ICE BOX MICKYLEE (hybrid, 80 days) puts out 7- to 10-pound (3–4.5 kg), 9- to 10-inch (23–25 cm) round fruits of 12 percent sugar content on 10-foot-long vines. These very productive plants do well in the North.

BLACKTAIL MOUNTAIN (hybrid, 70 to 75 days) was developed in northern Idaho, so you know it's suitable for northern gardens and/or cool temperatures, but it also does well in hot, humid areas. Round, dark green, 9-inch (23 cm) fruit, weighing on average 5 or 6 pounds (3 kg), raise the bar for taste in mini-watermelons. Sweet, juicy, crisp, and reliable, too!

Yellow Flesh

Yellow-fleshed melons are growing in popularity, both as a stand-alone treat and as an attractive addition to fruit salads and other recipes. The taste is much improved over that of early varieties.

Melons don't ripen after harvest. Some, such as North American cantaloupes, will get softer or juicier, even change color, but they do not improve in flavor.

EARLY MOONBEAM (OP, 80 days) is a sweet, early, productive little watermelon (5- to 8-pound [3.5 kg] fruit) with crystalline yellow flesh. A proven producer in the North.

SWEET SIBERIAN (OP, 80–85 days) produces extremely sweet, juicy, 8- to 10-pound [4 to 4.5 kg], oblong-shaped, light green fruit with apricot-colored flesh.

YELLOW DOLL (F1 hybrid, 68 days) is one of the earliest yellow-fleshed types you can grow. Fruit averages 7 pounds (3 kg) and the flesh is very sweet.

Exotics

Exotic watermelons run the gamut from unexpected colors to surprising flavors and are just as likely to turn up in small, easily trellised varieties as in mammoth ground sprawlers. Why not weave something a little different among your watermelon vines?

GOLDEN MIDGET (hybrid, 70 days) is a good-producing variety that is something of a shocker when ripe. The rind turns a vivid gold, while the ultrasweet, flavorful flesh matures to a deep salmon pink. Introduced in 1959 (like the author).

WHITE WONDER (OP, 80 days) produces delectable, small (3- to 8-pound [1 to 3.5 kg]) round melons, but the kicker is the soft, snow white flesh. Common in the 1800s, white-fleshed melons are now a rare treat. They will crack if overhandled.

Seedless Watermelons

Seedless varieties deserve our attention and respect, if not our outright admiration.

Developed through years of experimentation, these varieties provide superior vigor and disease resistance along with scrumptious, seedless fruit. Some varieties require

THE SECRET LIFE OF MELONS

Melons have the same sort of sexual identity crises as cucumbers, but most cultivars available for home gardeners are **monoecious** (both male and female flowers present on each vine). Male flowers bloom first, and since pollination depends on insects visiting both male and female, success is a matter of timing.

If fruit fails to set, or if you just want to make darn sure pollination is complete, try hand pollinating. Hand pollination is best done between 6 and 9 a.m. by collecting the male flowers and gently rubbing the anthers onto the stigmas of the female flowers. Seedless watermelons require pollination from an entirely different plant, so be sure to plant a pollinator variety nearby.

a (nonharvestable) floriferous pollinator be planted with them in order to set fruit.

BIG TASTY SEEDLESS (hybrid, 85 days) is a taste-test winner with sweet, firm, crunchy, red flesh and gray/green skin. Fruit averages 10- to 12-inches (25–30 cm) across and 6 to 8 pounds (3–3.5 kg) apiece. It holds its taste and texture for a long time after cutting.

SNACK PACK (hybrid, 75 days) proves good things come in small (3- to 4-pound [1.5–2 kg]) packages. Thin, dark green skin surrounds crisp, bright red, intensely sweet, chin-dribbling flesh. Requires a pollinator (provided by the seed company).

Never use products that contain sulfur on or near cantaloupes. Compost or rotted manure, worked shallowly into the soil just as the vines begin to flower, will aid fruit set.

SITE AND SOIL REQUIREMENTS

Melons are sun worshippers. To convert heat and sunshine into that sweet, succulent flesh, they need 8 to 10 hours of direct sunlight every single day.

Melons are also heavy feeders. They prefer a deeply worked soil, rich in organic matter, with a pH level between 6 and 7.5. Good drainage is essential. In heavy soil, raised beds will enhance drainage, as will adding organic matter. Compost or rotted manure added before planting time will get the seedlings off to a good start. Adding bonemeal, about

Once established, most melons grow prolifically, given enough sun and the right amount of water.

½ cup per foot of row, will help to promote early root growth. Cantaloupes are affected by boron-deficient soils; add granite dust to compensate.

PLANTING GUIDELINES

Melons are very tender plants and require 70 to 90 days of absolutely frost-free weather to reach maturity. In short-season climates, seeds need to be started indoors two to four weeks prior to transplanting. Like their cucumber, squash, and gourd relatives, melons are quite fussy about transplanting and do best started and transplanted in biodegradable pots so that the young roots are disturbed as little as possible.

Start two to four seeds per pot, and keep them moist and warm. When true leaves sprout, cut out all but the best plant per pot. Harden them off before transplanting (see Appendix 4) and be sure to wait until the soil is warm (70°F [21°C]) to transplant. Set the seedlings into the ground in their peat pots, and bury them so that no part of the pot is showing.

Direct seeding can be done only when the soil is warm and all danger of frost is past. Plant in hills, in raised beds, or in well-worked rows along a fence or trellis. Growing in vertical space means that even the most sprawling melons can be grown more closely together than in conventional hills or rows.

Plant four to eight seeds per hill, 2 to 3 inches (5–7 cm) apart and ½ inch (1 cm) deep. Hills should be spaced 4 to 6 feet (2 m) apart. If planting by rows, sow the seeds every 6 to 12 inches (15–30 cm) in rows 6 feet (2 m) apart. Thin to one plant every 12 to 18 inches (30–46 cm). Most melons will germinate in 7 to 14 days.

Watermelons need a little more space than other melons, so leave 18 inches to 2 feet (46–61 cm) between plants. They should come up in about 10 days.

SPECIAL TREATMENT FOR SEEDLESS SEEDS

Seeds of the hybrid, seedless watermelons are covered with a sticky, wrinkled seed coat that hinders the seedlings as they try to break through. They need special treatment to germinate, as follows:

★ Place seeds, pointed-end up, in moist seed-starting mix.

★ Keep them warm on a heating pad or cable until they sprout.

★ As soon as the infant plants poke through, gently remove the constricting seed coats.

★ Keep the young plants in a sunny window or under lights until transplant time.

Despite their large, juicy fruit, melons need only about an inch (2.5 cm) of water per week. But they need it consistently. Vines are most sensitive to lack of water between transplanting and just after flowering, when the fruit begins to set, and, of course, they need extra water during very hot spells. Water by drip hose or sunken containers to avoid the waste and possible disease spreading of overhead sprinkling.

Overwatering or a deluge following a long dry spell can cause the fruit to crack. Avoid this by allowing the soil to *almost* dry out between waterings. About two weeks before harvest, cut back the water. This tells a plant that it is time to stop enlarging the fruit and time to start concentrating sugar into it.

Melons can be tricky to finish in areas with short or cool growing seasons. To improve your odds, choose a short-season variety, start the seeds indoors, work plenty of organic matter into the soil, prewarm the soil with plastic and keep it on after planting, and cover the vines with floating row covers or even plastic sheeting until all danger of cool weather (50°F [10°C] or cooler) is past.

TRAINING MELONS TO GROW UP

A sloping support with a mesh at least 6 inches (15 cm) square is ideal for melons. A 2×4 A-frame or slanted fence with wire-mesh fencing or 1×2 wooden slats for plant supports is perfect (see page 27). Just be sure the trellis or fence you build is tall enough for the length of the vines and sturdy enough for the weight of the melons. Melons also grow well on a stout tepee with the slings tied to ropes wrapped around and between the legs.

Melon vines don't naturally climb on their own, so as the vines grow, they need to be guided to the support and then gently tied in place with soft cord or cloth. Some growers recommend pruning off the first side shoots until the main vine is growing well up its support, then managing the number of side shoots allowed to grow from the main vine.

As your melons grow, remove any flowers or fruit that form late in the season (within 50 days of your first frost date). They will not have time to ripen and will drain the plant of energy that is needed to mature those that set earlier.

Also, consider trimming back fruits to the best per vine. The more fruits that ripen all at once on the same vine, the less sweet they will be because the plant has to split the sugar it produces among them. Don't, however, remove leaves. They are the photosynthesis factories of the plant and thus the source of sugar production.

Using Slings

Vines that support the weight of fruit will grow stronger than those that just loll about on the ground, and the stems will also be stronger. Even so, climbing vines will have their breaking point, so larger melons require a bit of trellis customizing.

A fence serves double duty as a boundary and a support system for watermelons, making the most of a small yard.

Any fruit that reaches more than 3 or 4 pounds (1.5 kg) should be supported by individual slings. Cheesecloth, old panty hose, plastic-mesh vegetable bags, feed-sack cloth, torn-up sheets, and last year's bird netting can all be recycled for the task. However, solid fabric, such as an old T-shirt or pillowcase, has the added benefit of shielding the fruit from insect damage and sunscald as it grows, if you live in an area with intense sun.

Cut the material to fit the mature size of the melons that you are growing, with enough fabric left over to tie it to the trellis. To form a sling, secure one end of the cloth to the trellis, drape the midsection of it underneath the fruit, and then tie the other end to the trellis.

CHAPTER 11

SWEET

POTATOES

If the idea of climbing potatoes seems a little odd, you are probably thinking of plain, starchy Irish spuds, not these sweet tubers from sunny climes. Sweet potatoes (*Ipomoea batatas*), however, are members of the morning glory family, a clan well known for its climbing ability.

Native to Central and South America, sweet potatoes definitely favor a hot, moist climate. Traditionally, they have been a mainstay in gardens and commercial fields of the American Southeast, but they are by no means restricted to the South. With a little luck, a few trade-offs, and a lot of care and know-how, they can prosper well into the North. They have been grown successfully, often producing better yields in the nearly pest-free environment of middle and high latitude plots, as far north as New Brunswick, Canada.

VARIETIES

When it comes to sweet potatoes, most of us are familiar with two types: those deep orange, moist roots chronically misrepresented as "yams" in the grocery store and the light yellow, drier-fleshed versions. Thus, it may come as a surprise to learn that the International Potato Center, in Peru, has a collection of more than 6,500 varieties of sweet potatoes from around the world. That's gonna take a lot of marshmallows!

In North America, there are fewer than two or three dozen sweet potato varieties under cultivation. They differ in skin color from tan or yellow to orange, red, and even purple; in flesh from moist and soft to dry and firm; in flavor from subtle to sugary; in shape from long and tapered to blunt-nosed; and in growth time from 80 days to 120 or more.

There are even varieties with better natural pest resistance than can be achieved with chemical pesticides.

The best news is that even though sweet potatoes are decidedly hot-climate vines, excellent varieties thrive in cooler regions. And if you happen to garden in the South, you have your pick of the entire lot! Here are a few to consider.

GEORGIA JET (90 days) is a fast-growing (up to a foot [30 cm] per *day*) vine relished almost as much for its productivity (two and a half times as much as standard varieties in New York field tests) as for its great taste and moist, deep orange flesh. The skin is purplish red. It is cold tolerant (for a sweet potato), but in wet soil it is prone to cracking. Otherwise, it stores well and is readily available from suppliers.

Often grown as an ornamental for its beautiful leaves and trailing vines, the sweet potato is surprisingly easy to add to the garden as a root crop.

BEAUREGARD (90–105 days) is another highly productive, fast-growing sweet potato suitable for both northern and southern plots. Roots are generally long, with copper-colored skin and moist, orange flesh. They are resistant to soil rot, white grubs, and cracking but susceptible to root knot nematodes. Not as strongly flavored as other varieties, but it stores very well.

> Until being replaced with the variety Covington, Beauregard accounted for about 80 percent of commercial production.

COVINGTON (110 days) is a new variety (2005) that is fast outstripping the previous standard because of its reliability, uniformity, and disease resistance. Its skin is a rosy color and the orange flesh is sweet.

CENTENNIAL (90–110 days) is probably the most familiar sweet potato in the United States. The heavy-yielding vines are resistant to fusarium wilt, but moderately susceptible to stem rot and internal cork and susceptible to several other pests. The vigorous trailing vines are a striking purple-red with light green leaves. The potatoes are orange-skinned with sweet, moist, tender, deep orange flesh. They hold their quality well in storage.

SOUTHERN DELITE (100 days) is a moist, orange-fleshed variety with dark copper-colored skin. The flavor is good; it is excellent baked. It yields and stores well, and produces lots of sprouts for propagation, but its true claim to fame is its natural pest resistance. Released by Clemson University in 1986, it is naturally resistant to insects and soil rot.

REGAL (105 days) is another moist, orange-fleshed variety savored for its baking quality. It produces lots of sprouts and has high yields, in part because of its naturally pest- and disease-resistant vines. It boasts excellent resistance to fusarium wilt and internal cork, as well as to a host of beetles, grubs, and wireworms.

GOLDEN SWEET (100 days) is a beige-skinned, yellow-fleshed variety with a light, buttery, sweet taste and texture. This vigorous-growing vine produces an abundance of thick, tapered spuds.

FRAZIER WHITE (90 days) is an heirloom variety with white skin and very sweet, dry flesh. An easy-to-grow variety with reliable yields.

WHITE YAM (110 days) is the oldest American-grown sweet potato. The flesh is as white and sweet as sugar with a dry texture. It makes a good choice for both southern and northern gardens, provided there is a long enough growing season.

OKINAWA or **HAWAIIAN** (110–120 days) is a slow-growing, demanding vine that produces a skimpy crop by comparison to the other varieties listed, but the sweet, delicate, distinctly purple flesh may be just that special touch you're looking for. Skin color is dull beige.

SITE AND SOIL REQUIREMENTS

Admittedly, the best site and soil in which to grow sweet potatoes is a plot of sandy loam somewhere in the Deep South. But even for those of us who garden in cooler climes, there are ways to emulate that ideal. Given the right conditions, sweet potatoes are an easy crop, especially in areas with lots of sunshine. They are very drought tolerant and love the sun.

Sweet potatoes do best in areas that have 100 days or so of consistent 80 to 90°F (27–32°C) heat, finishing the growing season with temperatures around 60°F (16°C).

If possible, prepare the soil bed two to three weeks before planting (or even the preceding fall) by working in lots of compost or organic matter and giving it time to mellow before transplanting. Sweet potatoes require excellent drainage, so building up the soil into raised beds or hills a foot (30 cm) or more high is helpful. (This practice also produces larger roots that are easier to harvest than those planted in trenches or at ground level.)

Sweet potatoes prefer light, sandy, semidry, well-worked soil, free of rocks or debris that can interfere with the developing storage roots. Their roots can grow as deep as 8 feet (2.5 m), but they will produce nicely in porous soil that is well worked to a depth of only 8 inches (20 cm).

They have a fairly high demand for phosphorus and potash and will fail to produce in soil with too much nitrogen; a plant sends out all vines and few, if any, storage roots in nitrogen-rich soil. A somewhat acid soil, with a pH of 5.5 to 6.6, suits them best.

SAM I YAM

Though they look similar, true yams and the sweet potatoes we call yams in North America are from entirely different plant families. The yam (Dioscoreaceae), grown primarily in Africa, is starchier and drier than the sweet potato (Convolvulaceae), with less nutritional value.

Sweet potato skin and flesh come in a rainbow of colors beside the familiar orange/orange combo. They are divided into "firm" and "soft" types, indicating the consistency of the flesh when cooked. The soft varieties are what we usually think of as yams.

PLANTING GUIDELINES

Sweet potato plants grow from vine cuttings, called slips, that form on the roots. You can order these through the mail or online and can occasionally find them in a garden center, but they are easy to start at home.

Use only the best roots to propagate seedlings because you want to pass along only the best traits to next year's crop. Be sure the roots that are selected for propagation came from plants that produced well: six uniform potatoes per plant is a respectable yield.

Starting slips from last year's crop is the easiest way to propagate new sweet potato plants.

Start slips indoors six to eight weeks before your last expected frost. One method is to set a sweet potato in a container with the narrow (proximal) end of the root tilted up; this end grew closest to the plant and is the one that will send up shoots. The other, or distal, end will sprout roots.

1. Fill the container with enough moist sand or light potting soil to bury the bottom half of the potato (or suspend the spud with toothpicks in a jar about half full of water) and set it in a warm place.

2. Keep it moist and quite warm, about 80°F (27°C). Placing the container on a heating pad or coil will regulate the temperature. In about four weeks, 10 to 20 new vines will emerge from the top of the spud.

3. When the shoots are about 6 to 8 inches (15–20 cm) tall and have at least six swollen leaf nodes, cut slips from the root. Do not be concerned about the slip's roots; a healthy slip will send out new roots when transplanted properly.

It's possible to start slips from grocery store spuds, but you can't be sure of the variety, health, vigor, or productivity of the individual cultivar being cloned.

Another method for starting slips is to cut the end from a growing vine, about 1 inch (2.5 cm) above the soil line, and root it in potting soil. Nurture the vine tip over the winter, and cut and root more slips from it. By the next spring, you can have many well-started sweet potato plants to set out.

And even though this is not supposed to work, one of the most common ways of starting slips is to leave a sweet potato in a warm place and forget about it. Even spuds left in the dark will slowly sprout shoots if they feel like it.

Sweet potatoes are incredibly tender, so transplant slips well after the last frost date for your area to avoid surprise frosts. Be sure that the soil is well worked and sufficiently warmed (about 70°F [21°C]).

Sweet potatoes will rarely flower and set seed in the garden, except in tropical areas.

The best method is to place them at a slight angle and cover them so only the growing tips show above the ground. This encourages the underground nodes to send out more roots, and the plants are more likely to survive and produce greater quantities of evenly sized potatoes than are those that are planted vertically.

Space the slips 12 to 15 inches (30–38 cm) apart and water well. They are guaranteed to wilt soon after planting, but most spring back within three days. Since you can't harden off the slips, cover them at night with a bucket, Wall O' Water, or supported row cover to protect them from wind.

Once in the Ground

Weed control is crucial, as the roots begin to swell within six weeks of transplanting. Conventional mulch is not recommended for preventing weeds because it cools the soil; only gardeners in very warm areas should mulch sweet potatoes with standard types of organic mulch. For cool-season gardens, black plastic mulch is recommended because it helps to heat the soil and extend the growing season while retarding the growth of weeds. Stretch the plastic tightly over the soil bed, anchor it in place, and cut slits into the plastic through which to plant the slips.

Watering sweet potatoes requires a bit of finesse. Water generously for the first two weeks after transplanting. Once established, the plants need about an inch (2.5 cm) of water per week, more in very hot weather. With adequate water, they can thrive in air temperatures from 65 to 100°F (18–38°C).

They tolerate drought well and, in fact, will crack if overwatered, especially later in the season. Long, stringy roots, instead of fat tubers, are a sign that the spuds were overwatered or that the soil did not have adequate drainage. Too-wet soil, especially if too cool, can cause the roots to rot in the ground. Three or four weeks before your first expected frost, begin to water sparingly.

BETTER THAN AN APPLE A DAY

Sweet potatoes are a nutritional gold mine. They are rich in carotene, which converts to vitamin A (a whopping 380 percent of the recommended daily allowance), and contain healthy doses of vitamin C, complex carbohydrates, and fiber. They also offer B_6, E, and potassium, all for fewer than 100 calories per ½-cup serving.

TRAINING SWEET POTATOES TO GROW UP

Sweet potatoes grow long, leafy vines. If left on the ground, they sprawl into a matted mass that not only chokes out weeds and holds in soil moisture, but also cools the soil, eats up ground space, sends down roots at every node, and makes harvesting a tightrope walk among the tangled vines. Training those ranging vines to grow up lets you enjoy the benefits while avoiding the problems.

Even though a trellis holds only the vine and not the crop, it still must bear considerable weight. A fence-type trellis with heavy wire mesh or an A-frame or tepee with extra-rope supports works well. Train the vines into the supports by weaving them in and out of the mesh or ropes. Tying may help, but is usually not necessary.

One advantage of preventing sweet potatoes from rooting at will is that it prevents them from establishing new batches of tiny sweet potatoes that sap strength from the plant and result in lots of little sweets along the stems and few, if any, good-sized spuds. Strip any side shoots that sprout along the first 10 inches (25 cm) of each vine to make sure that there are no ground-level contact points.

Sweet potato vines make an attractive screen when trained up a fence or trellis, making them a double-duty plant.

PART III

FINE PERENNIAL

Fruits

How often have we heard it said that time is a thief? Countless souls lament the passage of the years, but gardeners seem to experience it differently. We work with time, use it, in fact, need it, to see our efforts come to fruition — literally. What time takes from the gardener, though, it bestows upon the garden, for a truly wonderful garden is more than the work of the gardener, or earthworms, or even seeds, roots, and foliage. It is the result of time. And nowhere is that more evident than in the production of perennial vines.

We sit in salivating expectation for those first few fruits, nurturing, hoping, begging for just a few berries, grapes, or kiwis. For most vines, the first year is a sacrifice that brings no reward. For many the second year is a tease, producing a few fruits but not enough to fill those canning shelves.

And then comes that glorious third season and all the abundant years thereafter: A plant has established itself. Both the garden and the gardener have adjusted their preferences and routines to one another. And time finally rewards you with a real harvest.

It feels like a gift: Plant once and harvest indefinitely. Oh, to be sure there is maintenance involved, and depending on your crop and situation, that can be a bit laborious. But when you stroll through your garden on a warm summer evening and pick a sweet-tart berry, juicy grape, or tangy kiwi from a vine planted many years ago, you can't help feeling that it was just offered up by the vine. All it took was time.

CHAPTER 12

BLACK-BERRIES

Sweet, soft, summer memories of deliciously fragrant wild blackberries, dripping from spiny brambles, inviting yet defying, inspire many nostalgic gardeners to plant a patch of their own. Domestic versions of those wild vines offer many advantages over those well-remembered thickets, such as larger fruit, more berries, and fewer thorns.

Be forewarned: Blackberries can take over a garden patch unless properly managed, but the abundance of perfectly ripe fruit, offered over an extended harvest season, is hard to resist. Knowing which plants have which needs makes all the difference between a well-tended patch of luscious fruit and a runaway ramble of brambles.

VARIETIES

One of the first and most striking developments in the old briar patch was the advent of thornless varieties. Now there are even more exciting improvements, such as advancements in yields, time of ripening, chill requirements, and, probably most encouraging of all to gardeners in cold climates, the release of **primocane bearers** — blackberries that fruit on the current season's canes. Growth habit may be erect, semierect, trailing, or semi-trailing with thornless or thorny canes.

Erect-growth-habit varieties form more of an unruly bush than a sprawling network of vines if left unchecked. Erect blackberries have stiff canes and need less support and guidance than do the trailing varieties, but they still benefit from some training. Less vigorous in growth, they spread by producing new shoots from the roots. Both erect and semierect varieties are more cold hardy than are trailing types.

Trailing varieties are quite familiar to residents of the South and Pacific Northwest, as trailing vines grow wild in those areas. In fact, Himalaya (*Rubus armeniacus*) and Evergreen (*R. laciniatus*) have naturalized in the Pacific Northwest to the degree that they are invasive. Blackberries are vigorous plants that should be trellised if only as an act of self-defense. Suckers sprout from crowns that grow at the base of each cane and/or from the roots.

Often referred to as dewberries, this group comprises both thornless and thorny varieties. Marionberries, boysenberries, and loganberries are trailing blackberries (or hybrids between blackberries and raspberries) that are known by their variety name. Lots of species readily hybridize, so botanical names are generally the genus *Rubus* followed by the named variety, such as *Rubus* 'Chester Thornless'.

Blackberries are closely related to raspberries, but are more vigorous and productive. However, they are not nearly as cold tolerant. Gardeners in the extreme north may be frustrated by their blackberries' sensitivity to cold, while those in the Deep South must settle for a few varieties that do not require winter's cold to produce dormancy.

But for true blackberry lovers in most of the country, the many available varieties offer a summer full of mouthwatering berries. By planting a few different cultivars based on ripening time, you can enjoy fresh blackberries all season long.

Thornless Blackberries

Thornless varieties take the pain out of tending and harvesting blackberries. First introduced more than 40 years ago, they

A cup of blackberries offers a good dose of vitamin E and is an excellent source of fiber, vitamin C, vitamin K, and manganese. Not to mention that they are delicious in pies, jams, and right off the vine.

continue to improve as breeders develop them.

TRIPLE CROWN THORNLESS (semierect to trailing, Zones 5 to 9, USDA release) is named for its three "crowning" attributes: flavor, vigor, and production. Strong canes grow to about 5 feet (1.5 m) long and require trellising. Production is outstanding, reputed at 30 pounds (13.5 kg) of sweet/tart berries per plant. Fruit is large and produced over several weeks.

DOYLE'S (trailing, Zones 3 to 10) is reported to produce from 10 to 20 gallons (38–76 L) of very sweet, oversized berries per plant

NOT A TRUE BERRY

Technically, blackberries are not berries at all, but aggregate fruits made up of lots of tiny drupelets. A **drupe** is any fruit that contains a single seed surrounding by dense flesh and a skin, such as peaches, plums, cherries, and olives.

per season. Sugar does not convert until just ripe, so the underripe berries are unremarkable. Some detractors object to the variety's high price and question its claims of hardiness and production. The seeds may be too large for fresh eating, but the fruit is excellent for syrups, wines, and other processing. Reportedly disease-free, plants are shipped very small but take off enthusiastically once rooted.

Many varieties of thornless blackberries are patented, which means it is illegal for you to propagate them until the patents expire.

THORNLESS EVERGREEN (trailing, Zones 5 to 9) started out as a thornless natural variety with both male and female characteristics. It has become one of the most popular commercial varieties. Its trailing vines produce high yields of good-quality fruit late in the season to extend the crop. It tolerates heavy, poorly drained soils better than do other varieties.

CHESTER THORNLESS (trailing, Zones 5 to 9) is a semierect variety with very good cold resistance. It produces high yields of good-sized, high-quality, round, deep black berries that are extra sweet. They are excellent fresh, processed, or made into wine. This variety is a fast grower — canes can reach 10 feet (3 m) long in a season — that ripens late (July to mid-August). Canes are very resistant to cane blight.

OUACHITA (erect, Zones 5 to 9), pronounced "WATCH-it-taw," produces extra-sweet berries starting in mid-June and continuing for five weeks. Plants are highly disease resistant.

Thorny Blackberries

Thorny varieties are the old-fashioned berries that made these brambles famous in the first place. On average, their berries ripen two to three weeks earlier than thornless cultivars and are usually sweeter. Most are easily propagated by suckers from the roots.

Though relatively self-fertile, they produce best if there is a second plant nearby for pollination.

SOMETHING NEW

Prime-Jan and **Prime-Jim** (trailing, Zones 6 to 9) represent the newest and most exciting innovation in blackberry plant breeding. They produce fruit on the current season's canes (primocanes) as well as on second-year canes (floricanes).

This means they have the potential for both a fall (primocane) crop and a summer (floricane) crop once established, or for a single fall crop each year on new canes. They can even be grown as an annual in especially harsh winter climates.

They do not produce well in low-chill areas, however, such as the Deep South and southern California. Flavor/sweetness is good. Prime-Jan sports larger fruit than Prime-Jim, but in smaller yields.

Primocanes are disease resistant, but floricanes may be susceptible to double blossom (rosette), a fungal disease that prevents fruit development on infected flowers.

CASCADE TRAILING (trailing, Zones 7 to 9) is native to the Pacific Northwest. Vines can reach 20 feet (6 m) in length. Berries have that true wild blackberry taste and are smaller than cultivated varieties. When sold as female-only plants, a separate pollinator plant is required to set fruit.

CASCADE (semierect, Zones 7 to 9) is believed to be a cross between the loganberry and the wild Cascade Trailing. Fruit tastes like the latter but is larger and more prolific.

CHICKASAW (erect, Zones 5 to 10) bears loads of large, flavorful berries. One of the best producers among the erect varieties.

MARIONBERRY (trailing, Zones 7 to 9), named for Marion County, Oregon, where it was tested, is a cross between the trailing varieties Chehalem and Olallie. It is treasured for its heady aroma and intensely authentic blackberry flavor. Thorns are large and plentiful, and the plant is very productive with canes up to 20 feet (6 m) long.

BOYSENBERRY (trailing, Zones 5 to 9) is a tart, tangy, sweet-tasting berry with a mysterious past. Some consider it a blackberry/raspberry hybrid. Berries are large (up to 2 inches [5 cm] long) and deep maroon in color with a distinct flavor and fairly large seeds. They ripen over an extended period, up to two months.

SITE AND SOIL REQUIREMENTS

Known for taking over roadsides and vacant lots, blackberries can handle such a range of conditions, from poor soil to filtered sun, that you might not think site and soil conditions matter much to them. Think again.

Most blackberries are fair-weather canes. They grow best in temperate climates with a moderate amount of winter chill (200 to 700 hours). Cultivated varieties require full sun to produce at their best but will perform well in filtered sun or partial shade.

Be careful when choosing a site. A well-situated, well-maintained patch can produce for 15 or 20 years, so pick a spot in which they will thrive politely. When in full vine, they will shade nearby plants. If not properly maintained, they will spread prolifically.

Blackberries grow in almost any soil, provided it drains well; their deep root system makes them unhappy in shallow, wet, heavy soils. Adequate moisture retention is essential, however, because these plants generally ripen their juicy crop during the driest part of the season. Deep, light soil that is well amended with organic matter, such as is created by raised beds, is perfect.

Blackberries favor a slightly acid soil (pH 5.5 to 7). If at all possible, test the soil the fall before you plant and adjust accordingly. You can maintain this pH range and boost soil nutrient levels by providing moderate applications of rotted horse manure every other year.

> Although thornless varieties are generally self-pollinating, some thorny types require a second variety planted nearby to ensure pollination. Check with your supplier when purchasing.

The best preparation for planting is to amend soil the summer or fall before planting with generous amounts of organic matter. Compost (finished or not) or manure (rotted or semi-rotted) work wonders. Remove any weeds and avoid adding anything that will contribute weed seeds to the patch. Dig or till in well, and let the soil sit over the winter to mellow.

Planting Guidelines

Plants available through nursery catalogs or from garden centers are generally one- or two-year-old bare-root canes, though older bare-root or potted canes are also available. When purchasing, be sure to check that the plants you are buying are certified disease-free. Transplant early in the spring, three to four weeks before the last expected frost, or as soon as you can work the soil.

Keep the roots moist by wrapping them in wet towels or heeling them into a trench in the garden until you are ready to set them out. When you are ready to plant, follow these steps:

1. Dig a hole just deep and wide enough to accommodate the bundle of roots.

2. Prune off any damaged roots.

3. Position each plant so the crown is just at the soil level or very slightly below, then, holding it in place, fill the hole partway and adjust the roots and plant for depth.

4. Water deeply, and let the water penetrate into the soil around the plant roots to collapse any air pockets.

5. Fill in the hole, gently press in the soil, and water again.

Heavy mulch can minimize two serious blackberry problems: it helps conserve precious moisture and keeps down weeds. This is especially important, as weeds can harbor insects or diseases, and cultivation can disrupt temperamental roots and cause suckers to form.

A thick mulch can also help to prevent frostbite if winter temperatures dip too low. Some varieties are so tender that in cold

The key to a successful blackberry patch is choosing the right spot and providing proper support for the canes.

climates the vines must be taken down and buried under several inches of soil to prevent winterkill.

Blackberries benefit from foliar feeding, that is, spraying the leaves with fertilizer. Apply a low-nitrogen fertilizer that includes calcium phosphate and potassium, at half the recommended dosage every two weeks.

TRAINING BLACKBERRIES TO GROW UP

Blackberries do not exactly climb; they sprawl in all directions. While it is entirely possible to grow masses of blackberry vines without trellising, doing so is an open invitation to a garden takeover. Most vines sucker or root very easily and spread at an amazing rate.

Don't start blackberries where tomatoes, potatoes, eggplant, or peppers have been grown; the soil may harbor verticillum wilt and then vines will not grow.

Even erect blackberries, though touted as "needing no support," fare much better with a little guidance. Set up a clothesline trellis (see page 25) with a wire or two on either side of the bushes to hold them in place. You may tie the canes to the wires or simply allow them to grow between the wires.

Trailing varieties can be trained to any type of trellis that suits your needs. A simple double-stranded, fence-type trellis serves well. As the vines grow, loop or zigzag them along the wires. Tie them with soft cord at intervals, and position the vines so that they receive maximum sunlight and airflow. The vines can also be trained onto a wire-mesh or fence-type trellis, or up the sloping sides of an A-frame (see page 27).

Here are some pointers to keep in mind while establishing a berry patch:

★ Train vines only when they are young, green, and flexible.

★ Don't try to train vines in freezing weather, as they will be brittle and prone to breakage.

★ Prune off any broken vines below the break, as injuries are a point of entrance for pests and diseases.

PRUNING POINTERS

Blackberries send out vines, or canes, that live for two years. The vines sprout lateral fruit-bearing branches in their second year. (Primocane varieties also fruit on the current season's growth.) Once established, tip-prune the nonfruiting canes (except for primocane bearers) in the summer, when they reach about 48 inches (121 cm) in length.

Tip-pruning causes growth hormones to be released in the canes and stimulates new growth from lateral buds, which in turn increases the number of lateral, fruit-bearing branches. The most vigorous varieties benefit from having these lateral branches tipped back as well to keep the overall size of the plant within bounds.

Once they have fruited, the vines of nonresistant varieties are incredibly susceptible to pests and diseases, and even those that are resistant aren't necessarily disease-*proof*. The spent vines should be cut at ground level as soon as they have been harvested and then burned.

In late winter or early spring, remove any winterkilled canes and thin the plants to about four or so evenly spaced, strong, healthy canes per plant (or foot of row) spaced about 6 inches (15 cm) apart. These will be the bearing vines for the current season, so anything you cut back is that much less vine that will bear fruit.

As the plants get older, they tend to send up more shoots each year, so more thinning is in order. Fewer, sturdier canes will produce more and better fruit than would lots of spindly canes.

CHAPTER 13

RASP-BERRIES

Rare and precious rewards await the gardener who cultivates his or her very own raspberry patch. But what a precarious prize they are. These delicately sweet/tart berries, heavenly when fresh picked, rapidly lose their form and flavor. A mere overnight stay in the refrigerator can change them from marvelous to mushy. What's more, the plants are terribly susceptible to viruses, and they sucker so readily that they often threaten to overrun the garden.

Are such temperamental treasures really worth the trouble? You bet they are!

VARIETIES

Raspberries, though also not true berries (see page 105), differ from blackberries in that they pull free of the core when picked at peak ripeness. The white hull stays on the vine, while the hollow, delectable fruit drops into your hand with barely a touch.

The more or less trailing and freestanding types yield red, yellow, purple, or black berries. The major differences are between single-crop, summer-bearing varieties and double-crop, fall-bearing (or everbearing) varieties.

Summer-Bearing Raspberries

Summer-bearing raspberries produce one crop per season on two-year-old canes called **floricanes.** They don't fruit their first year in the ground. Ripening times go throughout the season, depending on the variety, with harvest usually lasting from four to five weeks.

Red varieties (*Rubus idaeus*) are what most folks think of when they think "raspberries," and as they are the most common, they are listed first, but all colors of the raspberry rainbow are represented here.

Raspberries are a favorite summer treat, best eaten the day they're picked. A few pints in the freezer, however, can recall those warm days months later.

CANBY (Zones 4 to 8) puts out medium-sized juicy, firm, light red berries with that wonderful true raspberry taste and aroma. Canes are thornless, vigorous, and practically immune to viruses and aphids, but yields are notoriously low, ripening in midseason. It prefers cool summers.

CASCADE DELIGHT (Zones 6 to 9) might be the answer to your raspberry prayers or it could break your heart, depending on where you live. It is one of the raspberries most sensitive to cold, yet due to its outstanding resistance to root rot, it flourishes in soils too wet for other varieties (good drainage is still recommended, however). Heavy yields of big, firm, intensely flavored berries continue for about a month.

LATHAM (Zones 2 to 8) is the one to pick if you need cold hardiness and demand loads of berries. Introduced in 1920 and cultivated in Minnesota, this die-hard, dependable variety can survive temperatures as low as −40°F (−40°C). It falters only in areas with humid summers. Canes are upright, vigorous, and nearly thornless. Berries are large, fairly good-tasting, and produced for several weeks, beginning in midseason.

NOVA (Zones 3 to 8) is a close second to the above in hardiness, with superior, though somewhat tarter, flavor.

TULAMEEN (Zones 6 to 9) is the most widely grown fresh market red raspberry in the world for good reason. The flavor is excellent, though a bit unconventional; yields are high and produced over a long, late season; and berries are very large and attractive with medium red color and a glossy glow.

The long vines are easy to train and do well even in containers. It's resistant to raspberry mosaic virus, aphids, and powdery mildew. However, it's less cold hardy than most varieties and susceptible enough to root rot that it demands excellent drainage in order to grow.

AMBER (Zones 4 to 8) produces large yellow berries that mature fairly late. They are especially good fresh but also freeze well. Canes grow to 6 feet. Plants are susceptible to leaf curl virus. In general, yellow raspberries are hard to find, as most are poor performers.

Black Raspberries

Black raspberries (*Rubus occidentalis*), also called blackcaps, are summer-bearers only. They are less cold tolerant than red raspberries, grow in separate hills or clumps that do not spread out (or sucker) from the roots, and sprout canes that arch toward the ground. The cane tips can propagate new plants if allowed to reach the soil and root.

Plants don't live nearly as long as red varieties, yields are lower, and plants are more susceptible to diseases. The berries are often smaller, with more seeds, than red varieties, but they are often even more flavorful. That, and discoveries of their potent antioxidant content, keeps us growing them.

MUNGER (Zones 5 to 8) was released in 1890 and is still the most commonly grown commercial black raspberry. The fruit is medium-sized, shiny, blue-black, and firm with few seeds and good flavor. It's so-so for freezing but excellent for jams and jellies. Plants are moderately vigorous, require well-drained soils, and are quite resistant to fungal diseases. Bears in midseason.

JEWEL (Zones 4 to 8) is a Cumberland-type raspberry, meaning that it's everbearing, though truly it's a repeat bearer. The plants are vigorous, growing to 7 feet (2 m) tall before the canes arch over. They are more productive in temperate areas; berries ripen from early summer through fall. More disease resistant than most black varieties, Jewel is also longer lived. The glossy black berries are of excellent quality, large, firm, and very tasty.

BRISTOL (Zones 5 to 8) is another oldie but goodie, introduced in 1934 and growing strong ever since. The glossy black berries are presented in tight clusters. They are very firm, making them popular for freezing and processing, with a distinctively different flavor that has won it many a taste test. Growth habit is upright, so training required is minimal.

Fall-Bearing Raspberries

Fall-bearing (primocane) raspberries are sometimes called "everbearing," as they can produce two separate waves of berries each season. The first crop covers the bottom two thirds of two-year-old canes (floricanes) in late spring to early summer; the second ripens in late summer or fall (with some varieties producing right up until frost) on the top third or so of the current season's canes (primocanes). The following year, the lower two thirds of these canes will produce the early crop.

Most do not perform well in areas with a hot summer. Primocane varieties are red or yellow.

Red Fall-Bearing Varieties

Red fall-bearing varieties are the most commonly grown and the most popular of the fall-bearing varieties. Most people think they have the best, most "raspberry" flavor.

PURPLE RASPBERRIES

Purple raspberries are also summer-bearers. The results of red and black raspberry crosses, they have the same growth habit as black varieties. Most varieties are generally considered to be only so-so for fresh eating but excellent when processed. Hybrid vigor makes for more vigorous and productive plants than either red or black varieties.

Brandywine (Zones 4 to 9) berries have a rich, appealing aroma and a wonderful, sweet/tart red raspberry flavor that is prized for pies. When ripe, the huge, soft fruit takes on a deep purple color.

Royalty (Zones 4 to 8) berries mature first to a classic raspberry red with a familiar raspberry flavor and aroma. When fully ripe, they turn a dark, dusky purple with a distinct, excellent sweet taste and perfume. The soft fruit is large to very large and borne on vigorously growing vines.

HERITAGE (Zones 4 to 9) was once the standard to which all other varieties were compared. It produces high yields of medium-sized, firm, bright red, mild-flavored fruits in June or July and then again in September from stiff-caned, 6- to 7-foot-tall (1.5–2 m), easy-to-grow plants that excel almost anywhere. Though somewhat disease resistant and vigorous in growth, its late ripening gives it a short fall growing season. Berries stay firm even when past ripe.

> Raspberries are self-pollinating, but having more than one plant increases crop yields.

CAROLINE (Zones 4 to 10) outproduces every other everbearing red raspberry. Not only are yields bigger than other varieties, but so are the rich red, intensely flavorful berries. Though the canes grow to only about 4 feet (1 m) tall, they are vigorous, widely adaptable to different soils and climates, and resistant to root rot. Ohio State University studies have shown Caroline to be higher in antioxidants and vitamins than other varieties are.

RED WING (Zones 4 to 8) is similar to the old standard Heritage but ripens about two weeks earlier if cultivated as a fall-only crop. Berries are a bit larger, a tad softer, and of excellent flavor, fit for processing or fresh eating. Plants grow to about 6 feet (2 m), are winter hardy yet heat resistant, and can even do well in hot, humid weather.

Yellow Fall-Bearing Varieties

Yellow fall-bearing varieties are a mutation of red raspberries that inhibits the development of red pigment. The growth habit and fruit production are like those of red raspberries, but yields are typically lower and the fruit a bit softer.

FALL GOLD (Zones 3 to 8), once the, um, "gold" standard of yellow-fruited raspberries, it produces medium-sized, soft, delicately sweet, golden yellow berries. Canes are moderately vigorous, rapidly spreading, and very winter hardy. Production is moderate at best in warm, dry areas; it fares poorly in cool, damp climates and is susceptible to viruses.

KIWIGOLD (Zones 4 to 7) is a naturally occurring mutation of Heritage that was found in New Zealand in the mid-1980s. Plants are much more productive than Fall Gold, have a growth habit like Heritage, and are disease resistant. The fruit is a glowing yellow, medium-sized berry and has good to excellent eating quality and flavor. In blind taste tests, most testers could not distinguish it from Heritage. The fruit holds its shape better than other yellows and has a longer shelf life.

> Red and yellow raspberries will produce for 15 years or better; blacks and purples for up to 8.

ANNE (Zones 4 to 10) is considered by many to be the top pick of yellow-fruited raspberries and is often voted best-tasting. Its bright yellow, large berries are moderately firm and of excellent flavor. Production is medium to high, with berries ripening in June or July and then again in September. Plants are widely adapted to different areas and very dependable.

SITE AND SOIL REQUIREMENTS

Red raspberries flourish wherever apple trees thrive, whereas black raspberries love peach country. This is probably due more to climate than to soil. A cold winter and a dry, sunny summer is all that most varieties require. They prefer full sun in most areas, but if afforded some shelter from strong afternoon rays in hot areas, they will do all the better.

Berry patches that are situated along the east side of a building or fence fare very well, as they are shielded from the harshest sun. Planting at the top of a slope facilitates both water and air drainage. Cold air moves down the slope, away from the plants, reducing winterkill.

Choose a site cleared of perennial weeds, as weeding among the shallow roots causes them to send up shoots at the expense of the main plant. Do not plant where raspberries or other caneberries, potatoes, tomatoes, peppers, eggplant, or strawberries have been grown within the last three years, as those plants can harbor verticillium wilt and other diseases.

All raspberries prefer a mellow, aged soil and good drainage. The plants also appreciate a high content of organic matter. A slightly acid to neutral pH level (6 to 7) is ideal.

PLANTING GUIDELINES

In most areas, raspberries should be planted in early spring, but the job really begins the previous fall. Prepare a bed 2 feet wide by 1 foot deep (60 by 30 cm) to whatever length you have designated as the raspberry patch. Begin by removing the soil and, if you want to bother, lining the trench with planks or weed cloth to prevent underground suckers from sneaking out.

Shovel in a few layers of compost or manure, alternating with soil, and mix well with a spading fork. Top with another layer of compost or manure about 6 inches (15 cm) deep until the trench becomes a raised bed. Let the soil rest until spring, when it will be in prime condition for planting.

If you must prepare the soil in the spring, do it as early as possible to give the soil a chance to mellow, and use only aged compost or manure. In most areas, red raspberries can also be planted in the fall.

Orient rows in a north–south direction to allow for the maximum amount of sun exposure, a key to producing superior fruit.

Raspberry plants are available online, through mail order, and from local nursery outlets. The advantage to buying locally is that you will most likely be offered varieties that have been proved in your area. Online or mail order, on the other hand, gives you a lot more choice and freedom to experiment. Your local nursery owner or extension agent can give you regional advice. Be sure to insist on plants that are certified virus-free.

The plants will be shipped from early to mid-spring. Keep the roots moist until the ground can be worked. Before planting, prune the canes to 9 or 10 inches (23–25 cm) above the crown.

Proper spacing is critical to optimum production. Red and yellow varieties should be 18 inches (46 cm) to 3 feet (1 m) apart, in rows at least 5 feet (1.5 m) apart. Plant black and purple varieties in rows 6 to 8 feet (2–2.5 m) apart and about 3 feet (1 m) apart within the rows; they will form clumps to fill in the

For raspberries, yield increases of up to 50 percent have been reported on test patches using a V-shaped trellis like the one on the right.

space. Because of black raspberries' susceptibility to disease, never plant red and black varieties together — experts recommend at least 300 feet (91 m) apart.

Set the canes in the ground so the crown is at ground level and the roots are spread out evenly, then carefully backfill the hole. It's a common mistake to plant raspberries too deep. Be sure that the buds close to the roots are not covered; they are the future of the plants and need exposure to sunlight to grow.

As for food and drink, the raspberry patch will benefit from a topdressing of aged manure or compost every other year and about an inch (2.5 cm) of water per week. Mulching retains moisture, helps to keep cultivation to a minimum, and reduces the chances of sucker-prone roots. Late-summer or early-fall hoeing helps to disrupt soil-dwelling pests.

TRAINING RASPBERRIES TO GROW UP

Although stiff-caned raspberries are often sold with the claim that they need no trellising, they benefit from some guidance, and trailing varieties are doomed without it. Set up your trellis at planting time, and choose a design that suits both the berries and the site. A fence-type trellis, for example, fits nicely into a narrow space or even against a wall.

The very best design for raspberries is the V-trellis, which was developed by plant scientists at Cornell University. It is similar to a clothesline-type trellis, but the top wires are spaced farther apart than the bottom wires.

MOVING ON

Raspberry patches seem to decline every few years; most often this occurs because viral diseases get established. When this happens, it is time to relocate the patch. This can be done by allowing suckers to grow and digging them out or by tipping trailing varieties.

It is better, though, to start fresh with all new, certified disease-free stock rather than risk starting a new patch and finding it infected. This new planting also eliminates the risk of violating the patent on protected varieties.

The results are twofold: top-heavy, fruit-laden canes (they will produce right up to the very tips) can lean over the upper wires (protecting them from damage from their own weight or the wind), while new shoots can rise in the open center to more sunlight and better aeration than in other trellis systems.

The V can be set up in at least two ways. The first way is similar to the clothesline trellis, with two crossarms instead of four.

1. Set sturdy posts every 20 feet (60 m).

2. Cut the top crossarm 3 feet (1 m) long and the bottom crossarm 2 feet (60 cm) long.

3. Attach the shorter crossarm about 2½ feet (75 cm) up and the longer one about 5 feet (1.5 m) high.

4. Fasten heavy-gauge wires to each end of each crossarm and pull tight. Attaching one end of each wire to a turnbuckle will enable you to control wire tension over time.

You can also use 8-foot (2.5 m) steel fence posts.

1. Drive the posts 1½ to 2 feet (45–60 cm) deep in pairs set 1½ feet (45 cm) apart and angled away from each other at about 15 degrees from vertical. The tops of the posts should be spread about 3½ feet (1 m) apart.

2. Space the pairs of posts about 4 feet (1.25 m) apart, then drive an anchor post at each end of the row.

3. String one wire about 2½ feet (75 cm) from the ground and the other about 5 feet (1.5 m) up.

Like blackberries, raspberries are perennial plants that produce biennial vines, called primocanes, in their first year of life, floricanes in their second. Summer-bearing (floricane) varieties will bear fruit (at least a little) in their second season, and everbearing types will put out a crop in their very first fall.

Pruning Tips

The vines are pruned differently depending on if they produce a single summer crop on floricanes or yield double harvests (floricanes in summer, primocanes in fall). Restricting everbearers to only a fall crop is the simplest method.

Just mow them down with a lawn mower after they go dormant or the following spring. Doing so eliminates the early crop and forces the plants to concentrate on producing a bigger, better fall crop.

This practice also eliminates problems with flower-killing spring frosts, winter damage to fruiting canes, and diseases. It makes the fall crop come on a bit earlier and produces sweeter, more vibrantly colored fruit than that produced in the heat of summer.

Pruning summer bearers is a little more involved. The biennial vines produce fruit in the second season. New shoots come up during the summer as replacements for those vines that are currently in production. Keep these new shoots thinned as previously described.

As soon as the bearing vines (floricanes) are harvested (usually late summer), remove them to prevent diseases. At this time, the new canes (primocanes) can be tied in place. The following spring, cut out any winter-killed or damaged canes, then thin them to the best six to eight live canes per plant.

CHAPTER 14

STRAW-BERRIES

Strawberries utterly define the joy and angst of a love/ hate relationship. They are deliciously sweet and succulent, nutritious, versatile, cold hardy, and easy to grow, yet so much can go wrong. Strawberry disasters can include temperature-sensitive crop failures, bland fruit, slugs, nematodes, hordes of yellow jackets, thieving birds and mammals, rot, and sprawling, out-of-control growth. They make us hate them and let us love them, all in one bite.

Wild strawberries (*Fragaria* spp.) have grown in temperate climes since before recorded history. They were cultivated by the Romans at least two centuries BCE, and Native Americans had been growing them since well before the arrival of Europeans. When *F. chiloensis* (of Chile and western North America) and *F. virginiana* (of eastern North America) were introduced to Europe by New World explorers, the resulting cross, *F.* × *ananassa*, ignited a medieval strawberry craze.

Plant several varieties of strawberries to ensure a larger crop over a longer season.

VARIETIES

Species and interspecies hybrids of strawberry plants number more than 20, but those most commonly cultivated in Europe and North America today are *F. × ananassa*. Though hundreds of varieties exist, there are essentially only three types:

★ June bearing, which produce one large flush of berries, usually in June

★ Everbearing, which produce an early-summer crop, then a second flush in late summer or early fall

★ Day-neutrals, which keep chugging out berries all season long

Check with your local nursery to find out which varieties excel in your climate.

June Bearers

June-bearing varieties are the most popular of homegrown strawberries. They are famous for producing nice, big, juicy berries. Fruit sets over a 10- to 14-day period and ripens progressively over the next couple of weeks. Within that time frame there are subdivisions.

Early-season types are usually harvestable by late spring, **midseason varieties** about a week later, and **late-season types** about another week after that. (Some are even classified as early midseason, late midseason, and very late season, just to fill in any gaps in your June vacation plans.)

By growing strawberry plants that mature in different parts of the season, you can extend the harvest over several weeks. The biggest drawback to growing June-bearing varieties in containers or baskets is that they tend to send out a lot of runners that steal energy that would otherwise go into fruit production.

Early Season

EARLIGLOW (Zones 3a to 9b) is considered by many the tastiest of all strawberry cultivars. Berries start out large and firm with excellent flavor but become smaller toward the end of the harvest. Plants produce runners freely and are resistant to red stele root rot and verticillium wilt.

SABLE (Zones 3 to 8), from Nova Scotia, tastes as good as Earliglow or even better, and sets fruit slightly earlier. Berries are smaller and somewhat soft, and since flowers open early, frost can be a threat unless plants are covered.

Early Midseason

HONEOYE (Zones 3 to 8) is a longtime favorite for its high yields of large, firm, tart berries. It's not disease resistant and produces a hefty number of runners.

A Cherokee legend credits the strawberry, after other berries had failed, with reuniting the First Man and Woman after a quarrel separated them.

Late Midseason

JEWEL (Zones 4 to 8) is a perpetual favorite for good yields of large, firm, flavorful fruit with a glossy sheen. It doesn't perform well in a cold site and is susceptible to diseases.

Late Season

LATEGLOW (Zones 4 to 8), released from the USDA, is the standard favorite late variety for its good-sized, bright red, firm, flavorful fruit. Plants are resistant to red stele and verticillium wilt and not overly vigorous in producing runners.

CABOT (Zones 4 to 8) from Nova Scotia, is known for large yields of exceptionally large, sweet berries. Plants are resistant to red stele but susceptible to crown rot. A best pick for home gardens in northern locales.

Everbearing

Never mind what the seed catalogs say, everbearing strawberries don't really produce fruit year-round, but they will bear two or three flushes of berries over the season, most often in June and again in late summer or early fall.

OGALLALA (Zones 3 to 8) puts forth big, fat, firm, gorgeous red fruit that tastes a lot like wild strawberries. The plants are tough, hardy, and fairly drought resistant.

OZARK BEAUTY (Zones 4a to 8b) is a classic berry for the South. It produces lots of runners, which do not produce fruit in their first year.

QUINALT (Zones 4a to 8b) is so eager to produce that it puts out berries on runners before they can take root, making them a great choice for a cascading basket or container. The flavor tends to wane in wet, cool weather, but the plants keep on producing bright red, if bland, berries.

Day Neutral

These are the true "ever bearers," as they start producing in midsummer and don't quit until hard frost. Since production is continual, there is no real flush of fruit, rather a trickle all summer long, which is great fun and a real treat but adds up to a lower overall yield than with June or everbearing types.

Some strawberry varieties are better suited to container growing than others — do your research before buying your plants.

TRISTAR (Zones 2 to 7) has been a standard choice for over 20 years. It is disease resistant and a vigorous grower, yet moderate enough in runner production to make it a good choice for containers. Berries are of medium size and tastier than most day-neutral types.

MARA DES BOIS (Zones 4 to 7; 9 in the West) is considered a gourmet berry with almost wild flavor. Aromatic and intensely flavorful, flower production rests during periods of high heat.

EVIE 2 (Zones 4 to 9), developed in England, is easy to grow (it's less heat sensitive than the others) and highly productive for day-neutrals. Berries are large, red, and tasty.

SITE AND SOIL REQUIREMENTS

Strawberries need at least 6 hours of direct sun per day in order to produce their best and biggest harvests. When planting in containers, position them where they will receive full sun or turn them regularly so that all sides receive adequate sunlight. Though they are not fussy about soil type, strawberries do best in well-worked, slightly acid (pH 5.8 to 6.5), fertile soils rich in organic matter. One thing they don't tolerate well is soggy soil.

Because they can share soilborne diseases, fungi, and insect pests, don't plant a new strawberry patch where an old strawberry patch, related plants (peppers, eggplants, and tomatoes), or sod have grown within the last three years. This includes containers — or more to the point, the soil from a used container. Also, since they bloom early in spring, don't position strawberries in low-lying areas, as these tend to collect cold air, which can damage or kill early blooms.

PLANTING GUIDELINES

Strawberries are versatile! They can be planted in hills, pyramids, beds, bags, barrels, baskets, pots, strawberry jars, a modified version of the potato tower, or even an old shoe organizer, provided they have enough room to develop healthy roots. The consensus among those who experiment with such things is that strawberries need about 8 inches (20 cm) of root space to perform well.

When planting, whether in containers or in the ground, leave plenty of space between plants — about 18 inches (46 cm) between June bearers and 8 to 12 (20–30) for everbearers and day-neutrals — in order for each to receive adequate sunlight and air circulation. Strawberries prefer not to be crowded. You're better off using specially designed strawberry pots or multiple containers with one plant each than to try and cram several plants into a larger pot.

Forget those ads hawking "climbing strawberries." Strawberries don't grow on vines or climb, so what they are most likely selling are varieties that put out runners on which fruit can develop without benefit of rooting, such as Quinalt.

The best time to plant is early spring. This gives plants time enough to establish themselves before the main growing season. If roots are longer than 4 or 5 inches (10–13 cm), trim them back before placing the plant in prepared soil. Carefully spread out the roots and gently press them into the soil with the crown (the juncture where the roots meet the stem) just above soil level.

TRAINING STRAWBERRIES TO GROW UP

Strawberry plants can easily live up to five years, but they generally start to produce fewer berries by their third year and decline thereafter. Nobody knows this better than the strawberries themselves, and they have come up with a solution. Strawberries propagate by sending out **stolons**, or runners — long, trailing stems, each with a small, immature

STRAWBERRY POTS FOREVER

Commercially available strawberry jars have a bad rap because so many of them are cheap, subpar knock-offs of a great idea. A well-made, well-designed strawberry pot, however, is a marvel of vertical-gardening engineering. When purchasing a strawberry jar, look for these features:

★ **Size.** Bigger *is* better. Consider a 3-gallon (11 L) jar with six to eight pockets the minimum.

★ **Large planting pockets.** Pockets smaller than 3 inches around are difficult to plant.

★ **Rimmed pockets.** These help to hold in soil, roots, and water.

★ **Material.** Ceramic is the best. Terra-cotta dries and wicks moisture away from soil. Plastic is usually too flimsy.

★ **Good design.** Look for an appealing shape, with pockets alternating around the circumference.

If there is a drainage hole at the bottom of the jar, cover it with pot shards to prevent soil from leaking out. If there isn't, drill one, or cover the bottom few inches of the pot with shards or gravel to enable excess water to drain away from plant roots.

To plant, fill the jar from the top with moist soil medium until it is flush with the bottom pockets. Place one plant per pocket, then fill soil to the next pocket level and repeat until the jar is full.

A self-watering system can be added to just about any container, or rig your own using a 1- or 2-liter plastic bottle, about the same height as your strawberry jar. Drill tiny holes along the length of the bottle, making four or five lines of holes.

Place the bottle in the center of the container, then fill the container with soil (and strawberry plants!), leaving the top of the bottle exposed. Fill the bottle with water, then cap. The water will slowly drip, watering all levels of the container.

daughter plant at the end. When these small plants contact soil, they send down roots, and voilà, a new plant is born. Garden strawberry patches are often managed by guiding these runners into new rows and systematically removing old plants every two or three years, leaving the new ones.

Strawberries need 1 to 2 inches (2.5–5 cm) of water per week, but good drainage is just as critical. Planting in hills, pyramids or towers, raised beds, or containers facilitates this nicely. Be aware, however, that containers can either dry out too quickly or become waterlogged, depending on the type of container and the irrigation/drainage setup. Keep soil damp, not soggy and not crumbly dry.

Depending on your soil mix, fertilizing may or may not be helpful. A high phosphorus fertilizer, added every other week while the plant is flowering (for June bearers, this means once or twice), will encourage plentiful blossoms. Too much nitrogen, though, can lead to all leaves and no berries.

Many people advise picking the flowers on June-bearing strawberries in their first year in order to allow the plants to establish themselves. It is believed that they will produce more abundantly in subsequent years as a result. In commercial settings, this is common practice, but it is generally not necessary in home gardens, as consumer transplants should be mature enough to handle rooting, growing, and producing in their first season. A similar strategy is used for freshly planted everbearing strawberries — blossoms are picked until midsummer to encourage a hefty fall harvest and improved harvests thereafter.

Once your strawberry plants are well established, it's easy to propagate another generation from the runners.

CHAPTER 15

GRAPES

Though not a common garden staple, a grapevine or two can become an undisputed star, even in a limited space. From beautiful, edible foliage that quickly grows to provide a privacy screen to bunches of delicious, juicy grapes, it has so much to offer. Since grapes are particular about their growing conditions and can take up to six years to produce a full crop of fruit, many gardeners do not think they are worth the effort. But to reach up and pluck a perfectly ripe, sugary sweet, homegrown grape from your arbor and pop it into your mouth is to be converted forever!

VARIETIES

Grapes are one of the oldest cultivated plants, first grown circa 8000 BCE by the Greeks and Turks, who considered them the "food of the gods." When Europeans discovered the vines, they became major crops in Spain, Italy, and France.

After Columbus brought wild Native American species back to Italy with him, viticulturists began hybridizing them, and since then, thousands of varieties have been developed. Grapes are classified as either table grapes (for fresh eating, juices, raisins, jams, and jellies) or wine grapes. Different varieties ripen at different times, making it possible for you to enjoy fresh grapes of different colors, tastes, and textures throughout the growing season.

Table grapes are tastier straight from the vine and may be seeded or seedless. They are categorized as red, white (sometimes green), or blue (to black), and have a fabulous range of tastes.

Wine grapes usually have seeds, are often smaller than table varieties, and come in much the same range of colors.

Based on their species' origins, both table and wine grapes are categorized as European

The ancient and often venerated grape has been part of human history for many centuries.

(*Vitis vinifera*) or American (also called "slip-skin" grapes, because they have a tough skin that peels off the berry easily).

European grapes include Muscat grapes, which have a distinctive, musky flavor and a sweet, floral aroma.

American grapes are subdivided by species. The most common are *V. labrusca*, which have a deep, musky, "labrusca" flavor, and Muscadine grapes, *V. rotundifolia*, with a somewhat lighter, fruitier flavor.

Many hybrids, including French hybrids, exist between *V. vinifera* and various American species. Because of their cold hardiness and ease of growing, most home-garden grapes grown in the United States are either American or French hybrids.

Muscadine grapes grow differently from other types. They are not cold hardy and require special pruning and trellising techniques, but they offer a great variety of colors and flavors in return. Many Muscadine vines require cross-pollination to set fruit, unlike the vast majority of grapes, which are self-pollinating.

Table Grapes

Table grapes come in dozens of varieties; choosing the one (or ones) that will fare best under your growing conditions is key to your success. Research varieties carefully before you buy and learn about providing their exact preferences, and you will be well rewarded for your diligence.

Seedless Grapes

Seedless varieties are the most popular table grapes, though some have seed remnants (a quality that can be affected by weather). Seedless grapes are generally less cold hardy than are seeded types.

THOMPSON SEEDLESS, also known as Sultanina (*V. vinifera*, Zones 6 to 9), is probably the most familiar table grape in the world. However, as a homegrown variety, it is included here mainly for comparison. It does very well in areas with a long, hot summer but flounders in cool weather. Vines are vigorous but cold sensitive. Cane pruning (page 131) and fruit thinning (page 128) are needed for it to produce the best fruit. Its oblong, light green berries are juicy, firm, and mildly sweet; they make excellent raisins.

INTERLAKEN (*V. labrusca* × *V. vinifera*, Zones 5 to 9) produces large clusters of small, golden green, fleshy berries of superb, sweet/tangy, labrusca flavor on vigorous, heavily productive vines. Excellent fresh or for raisins. Disease resistant, early-ripening, and recommended for mild climates.

MARQUIS (*V. labrusca* × *V. vinifera*, Zones 4 to 8) proffers very large clusters of large, round, yellow-green grapes with a melting texture and mild fruity taste that evolves into a strong labrusca flavor the longer they stay on the vine. Plants are moderate in hardiness, vigor, and productivity.

RELIANCE (interspecific cross, including *V. labrusca*, Zones 5 to 8) produces medium-sized, very sweet, labrusca-flavored, tender-skinned, pinkish berries. It is a good producer with some of the best cold tolerance found in a seedless variety, but berries don't always color up well and may crack in wet years.

CANADICE (*V. labrusca* × *V. vinifera*, Zones 5 to 8) produces excellent-tasting, sweet, red berries in long, compact clusters on vigorous, disease-resistant vines that are extremely productive when properly trained. It is cold hardy to –20°F (–29°C), but fruit rot can be a problem in wet years. Tends to overcrop (produce an abundance of subpar fruit).

VANESSA (interspecific cross, including *V. labrusca*, Zones 5 to 8) is an excellent quality red grape borne on moderately vigorous vines. Berries and clusters are medium-sized. There is a soft seed remnant, but the fruit quality is outstanding with a superior crisp texture and fruity flavor.

FLAME SEEDLESS (*V. vinifera*, Zones 6 to 10) has become the next favorite table grape after Thompson Seedless for its sweet-tart flavor and crisp texture. Berries are flame red to dark purple, round, and somewhat small. Vines are vigorous, growing to

BUYER BEWARE

One frustration in choosing the perfect grape variety to grow is that many are restricted by quarantine regulations (due to viruses and phylloxera) from being shipped to specific states. Be sure to check that the variety you want is available in your state.

20 feet (6 m) long. Clusters are open, which fosters crack resistance.

CONCORD SEEDLESS (*V. labrusca* with some *V. vinifera*, Zones 5 to 7) offers all the intense, deep flavor and juicy texture of the standard Concord, but the blue-black fruit ripens earlier. The berries are smaller and grow in smaller clusters than the seeded variety. Production can be erratic in some areas, but it is still considered an excellent choice for home gardens. Seeds may form in warm years. Vines grow to 15 feet (4.5 m) long.

> Technically, grapes are classified as berries, being a fleshy fruit produced from a single ovary.

JUPITER (interspecific cross, Zones 5 to 8) produces large, oval, firm berries of excellent mild Muscat flavor, early to midseason. Berries ripen from red-blue to blue, are fairly thin skinned and crisp, and resist cracking. Plants are moderately vigorous and very productive. Soft seed remnants are rarely noticed. Considered by many to be the best seedless American hybrid Muscat.

Seeded Grapes

Seeded varieties often have superb flavor, making them favorites for juices and jellies as well as fresh eating. Many have superior cold hardiness to seedless varieties, and a few are versatile enough to be used in wine-making.

CONCORD (*V. labrusca*, with some *V. vinifera*, Zones 4 to 9) is the most widely grown American grape. Cultivated since 1843, it grows in a wide range of climates and soil types. Vines are vigorous, disease resistant, and productive. A slipskin variety, the skins are thick and tough but separate easily from the flesh. The large, round, blue-black fruit has a deeply sweet aroma and sweet labrusca flavor; it is prized for juices and jellies. Fruit is somewhat prone to uneven ripening in warm climates.

STEUBEN (interspecific cross, Zones 4 to 8) is known for its pretty, tapering clusters of red-blue grapes. The vines are hardy, vigorous, disease resistant, and productive, making it a shoo-in for the home grower. The berries have a sweet-tangy taste, suitable for fresh use, juice, and wine.

MUSCAT HAMBURG (*V. vinifera*, Zones 5 to 8), also called Black Muscat, among its multiple aliases, is a blue-black, mid- to late-season table grape of outstanding quality and excellent sweet/tart flavor. Berries are oval and resist cracking but are inconsistent in size. Cane pruning (see page 131) is sometimes recommended. Also grown as a wine grape.

CATAWBA (*V. labrusca* with some *V. vinifera*, Zones 4 to 9) is another old-fashioned favorite, released in 1823 and relished ever since for its spicy, labrusca-flavored, slipskin berries. Grapes are red, crisp-fleshed, and very sweet and juicy. Vines are vigorous and productive though somewhat susceptible to downy mildew. Foliage is sensitive to ozone pollution.

SWENSON RED (hybrid including *V. labrusca* and *V. riparia*, Zones 4 to 9) adds the subtle taste of strawberries to the grape-flavor palette. Berries are firm, fleshy, and juicy, and ripen to dark red except in areas with cool nights, where they mature to a deep blue. Vines are hardy to –30°F (–34°C), improving in vigor and productivity as they age. Matures midseason. Highly susceptible to downy mildew.

GOLDEN MUSCAT (*V. labrusca* × *V. vinifera*, Zones 5 to 8) produces large clusters of

A well-tended grapevine can produce for decades, so give serious consideration to its location before you first set out the plants.

oval berries that mature from light green to amber late in the season. The sweet, tangy, citrusy fruit is of excellent quality.

EDELWEISS (interspecific cross, including *labrusca*, Zones 4 to 8) is an early-ripening green/white grape prized for fresh eating, juice, and jellies. Large clusters of medium-sized berries of high sugar content are also used in wines. Vines have excellent disease resistance, are hardy to –30°F (–34°C), and adapt to a range of soils and climates.

SITE AND SOIL REQUIREMENTS

Certain combinations of terrain, soil, and climate are more suited to grape growing than others. This is why some areas of the globe are renowned as "grape country." Although soil preferences differ somewhat among varieties, grapes are not dependent on rich, fertile soil. Some of the most successful vineyards in the world have been maintained for generations on weak-soiled, rock-strewn slopes.

Even though the vines will take root and grow in almost any kind of soil, most prefer a light, gravelly loam in order to set fruit. They will also do well in heavier soils, even clay, as long as there is sufficient gravel or rock to facilitate drainage. Most won't survive heavy, wet soil. With roots that extend to 8 feet (2.5 m) deep and more, grapevines demand good drainage and deep soil. Stones or gravel in the soil also help to hold heat during cool fall days.

Besides drainage, the most important aspect of your potential grape-growing soil is the site that it occupies. Grapes love a gentle slope and prefer to face the southeast or southwest, where they will receive full sun, especially when they are grown in northern gardens.

Some type of windbreak, such as a stand of trees at the base of the slope, helps moderate windchill. Flat plots are subject to unexpected frosts and still, stagnant air that may promote fungal diseases. Sunken areas, which usually have poor drainage, are even worse.

The other chief concern of the grapevine's location is the area's climate. New cultivars are hardy to −30°F (−34°C) or lower. Most grapes, however, luxuriate in long, lazy summers and warm autumns. They may suffer if winter temperatures dip below zero or if they are caught by a late-spring or early-fall freeze.

WE'RE NUMBER ONE!

Buy only healthy, large, 1-year-old, #1 vines. The number is an industry grade denoting the best plants.

Vines, roses, and other plants sold as bare-root are graded for size and health (according to their particular type) and labeled for sale. Number 1's are generally more expensive and have a larger diameter.

PLANTING GUIDELINES

The gardener who sets out new grapevines is committing an act of faith. The most important part of home grape growing has already been done — selecting the very best variety or varieties for the plot. The most that can be done now is to set this newcomer off to a good start.

Soils high in organic matter and nutrients can actually be detrimental to a grape crop. The vines tend to grow profusely but the woody parts do not mature, and fruit production is low and often of inferior quality.

Plant grapes in early spring while the vines are dormant or just beginning to form buds. This schedule gives them months of comparatively mild weather to establish strong roots before having to face the winter.

1. Begin by thoroughly working the soil in the planting area as deeply as possible. You may want to add some organic matter, sand, or gravel to improve drainage.

2. Once the bed is prepared, dig a hole deep enough and wide enough to accommodate the root mass.

3. Before setting the vine into the hole, cut away any damaged roots and prune the remaining roots to about 10 inches (25 cm) long.

4. Choose the strongest, best-looking cane that rises from the crown to be the central leader for the vine, then remove all the others. The central leader will be the trunk of the new grapevine. It, too, needs to be trimmed back, to two or three healthy buds.

5. Set the fledgling vine into the hole and add a few inches of good garden soil. Holding the plant near the crown, gently pull upward to let the soil settle around the roots. Fill in the hole and give the plant a good soaking. Once the water has drained, press the soil down firmly and add more soil if necessary.

Since most varieties are self-pollinating, you can plant a single vine if that's all you want or have room for. Spacing multiple plants depends on the growth habit of the vines you select; less vigorous vines should be planted more closely together to maximize yields, and more vigorous vines need extra space to avoid growing into one another.

TRAINING GRAPES TO GROW UP

Nothing rambles more freely than an unfettered grapevine. Left on its own, it will easily spread 50 feet (15 m), twisting, tangling, and *not* producing much fruit. Taming that free spirit is actually the secret to unleashing its bountiful potential.

Pruning and training to a support are critical to your grapevine's wellbeing and productivity. These techniques limit the burden the vine must support and nourish while maximizing sun exposure and air circulation. They are intricately connected; how you prune will depend, in part, on the training

THINNING OUT LEAVES AND FRUIT

Aside from limiting excess growth, two major considerations in pruning are sun exposure and air circulation. Sunlight affects not only how well fruit ripens, but also bud formation for next year's crop. Developing buds must receive sufficient sunlight in order to sprout the following year. Too much shade from a leafy canopy this year can lower the harvest next year.

Good air circulation is a real boon to bearing grapevines. Pests and disease organisms take refuge in the dense, moist canopy of the leafy vines. Although leaves are essential to the health of the plant and produce food from sunlight while shielding developing fruit from its intensity, lush dense layers of leaves also create the perfect microclimate for fungal diseases. Thinning a few leaves helps cut down on the potential for disease.

Fruit Thinning

It's also important to thin fruit. Leave only one cluster per new shoot in the third and fourth years. Thereafter, depending on the vigor of the variety, leave 16 to 20 bunches per plant. Remove any small or poorly filled-out flower clusters as they form. This measure causes the plant to focus on ripening the best fruit in the biggest bunches.

The earlier fruit is thinned, the better for the plant and the remaining fruit. Some varieties are so vigorous and set so much fruit that they overstress themselves. A condition called overcropping — overproduction of subpar fruit — can significantly weaken, even kill, a plant. Be sure to limit the number of clusters a plant is forced to sustain.

DON'T LEAVE OUT THE LEAVES!

Grape leaves are edible, so when pruning or plucking to open up the vines, save tender, medium-sized leaves. Cut off the stems, wash the leaves in clear water, boil, drain, and stuff with rice, toasted pine nuts, herbs, and ground or finely chopped lamb for a traditional Mediterranean entrée (dolmades).

system you use. Failure to properly prune and train the vines results in few, poor-quality, small grapes in small, unevenly ripening clusters — if you're lucky.

The growth habit of each variety dictates the type of trellis and training method best suited to it. American varieties tend to dangle from a main stem, so they do best on a tall trellis that allows the vines to hang down (without reaching the ground). European grapevines generally grow upward, benefiting from a low support with room to climb. The idea is to work with the nature of the vines.

Training Up an Arbor

Grapes are often pictured sprawling over an arbor for a wonderfully dramatic effect. The spreading vines should be trained up and then tied along horizontal supports. Design the arbor so that the supports are sturdy enough to hold up the bearing vines and fruit. If it's a large structure, it also has to be strong enough that you can safely climb up and work among the vines.

Once established, a grape arbor makes an unparalleled garden retreat. It may take several years for the trunk to reach the top of the

arbor. Until it does, keep removing any side shoots to encourage upward growth. Once it reaches its intended height, allow the vines to fan out over the arbor, training accordingly. This method is best suited to American-type grapes.

Constructing a Trellis

The traditional method for growing grapes is to train the vine along a wire, fence-type trellis, but you can construct a trellis of any material you like (wood, bamboo, rope) provided it is strong enough. It's best to install the trellis when the plants go into the ground, before roots have started to spread.

For a wire trellis, use 12-gauge or heavier wire, or high-tensile wire, strung tight, to hold the weight of branches and (hopefully!) fruit. Turnbuckles enable you to adjust and maintain the wire tension.

You will also need sturdy posts, at least 4 inches (10 cm) in diameter. These posts will be under considerable stress from the tension of the wire and the weight of the vines.

1. Bury 8-foot (2.5 m) posts about 2 feet (61 cm) deep, or use longer posts and bury them even deeper. You can make the posts more solid by anchoring them in concrete and/or by bracing each end post with a 4×4 post wedged into the ground. The end posts will bear most of the load and must be the sturdiest. Drive or set them into the ground leaning slightly away from each other.

2. Intermediate posts should be set every three vines, or along every 18 to 22 feet (5–6 m) of trellis. Heavy-duty metal fence posts may be substituted for wooden ones, but they must be well braced. Another alternative is to drive a steel support post into the ground next to each plant.

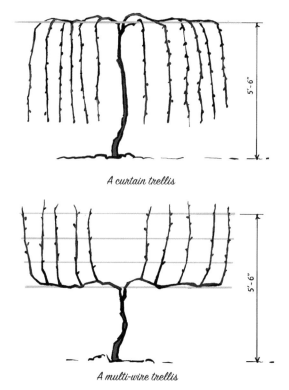

A curtain trellis

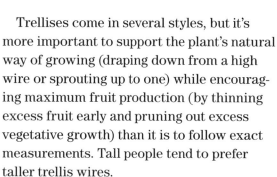

A multi-wire trellis

Head training

Trellises come in several styles, but it's more important to support the plant's natural way of growing (draping down from a high wire or sprouting up to one) while encouraging maximum fruit production (by thinning excess fruit early and pruning out excess vegetative growth) than it is to follow exact measurements. Tall people tend to prefer taller trellis wires.

Single-wire, or single-curtain, trellises, strung from 5 to 7 feet (1.5–2 m) high, are a good choice for American grapes. After the main trunk reaches the wire, one bud in each direction of the wire is chosen and then trained by tying the vine at intervals along the wire as it grows. The next season, a few buds are allowed to grow into shoots that hang from the underside of the arm. These will be pruned back each year to a few healthy buds (spurs), which will renew the process again each year.

Multi-wire trellises allow upward-growing vines (European and hybrid types) to climb to their heart's content. From two to four wires are typically used. Canes are trained upward by using a vertical line for them to follow to a top wire or by using several horizontal wires and weaving the shoots through them as they grow.

Head-training involves training the trunk up a stake until it hardens into self-supporting wood, then allowing shoots to grow out to the sides (either along a wire or radiating out and down from the top, like a weeping tree). Again, these shoots must be pruned back to the spurs each year to keep fresh wood forming.

PRUNING TIPS

The first objective of pruning and training newly planted vines is to encourage a healthy root system. Prune as described at planting time, then choose one shoot and, as it grows, train it along a stake or wire to grow straight up to form the trunk. Cut out all other shoots, but allow foliage to grow from your chosen one in order to sustain the plant and produce roots. If the young vine doesn't reach its intended height, repeat the process the next year. Remove any flower clusters that form the first year.

For the next two or three years, pruning focuses on conforming the vines to the trellis. Young vines aren't strong enough to support fruit, so be sure to remove any flower clusters that form in the second year. After the plant has reached its mature size and shape, annual pruning will be geared toward maintaining a healthy plant and ripening the largest, best-quality fruit possible.

Vine pruning should be done when the plant is dormant or almost dormant. Any time after the leaves fall in the autumn until the buds begin to swell the next spring is fine. Do not prune, however, when the wood is frozen, since brittle canes are easily broken or damaged.

There are two basic types of pruning: cane pruning, which generates a whole new arm (of year-old wood) each season, and spur pruning, which creates new spurs each year along an established arm, or cordon.

Cane pruning is commonly used for American varieties. It consists of pruning out all of the current season's wood after harvest, except for two new arms (and in some cases, two new renewal spurs) near the trunk, from which next season's new shoots will emerge. Cut through the last bud on the arm to prevent it from sprouting. Spur pruning is not recommended for American-type grapes or French hybrids, as they do not fruit from basal spurs as do *vinifera* (European) grapes.

Spur pruning is more suited for muscadine and many wine grapes. Because they set

> Once established, 75 to 90 percent of the previous season's growth should be hacked off. It's a little hard to get used to, but once you see the results, you'll know it's for the best.

fruit along short vertical shoots or spurs that rise up from the horizontal cordons rather than along the cordons themselves, they must be trained in a slightly different way.

You need only a single wire strung 30 to 60 inches (76 to 152 cm) above the ground. The central leader is trained up to the wire and a strong vine is allowed to grow from each side. These side branches are grown longer than in the other training methods to accommodate as many vertical shoots as the plant can sustain. These shoots are pruned to two or three buds, each of which will produce a cluster of grapes in the fall. After they produce, the spurs are pruned to make way for those that will bear the following year.

Regardless of the method of training used, grapevines set fruit only on current season's growth sprouted from 1-year-old wood; there must always be a few new vines growing to replace those in production. Most grapevines can reasonably sustain from six to eight branches, but too much growth or fruit production overtaxes the vine. Reduced yields and poor-quality fruit will result. Keep extra shoots trimmed, and remove any branches that do not set fruit along with the others. They may try to set fruit later, but the vines will probably not have time to ripen their load before frost. Promptly remove any dead and diseased vines whenever you see them.

CHAPTER 16

KIWIS

Melonettes anyone? How about a nice Chinese gooseberry or monkey peach? If you garden in a northern clime, perhaps you'd like to sample the fruit of the bower vine. These are but a few of the aliases of the seemingly ubiquitous kiwi, which originated in Southeast and Central Asia, where it has been cultivated since ancient times. It can still be found growing wild in some regions of China.

Once discovered by enterprising fruit growers, varieties began to travel and have prospered in areas as diverse as Italy, New Zealand, California, and New York, and just about all points in between. This comes as no surprise, because kiwis have it all.

There is a variety of kiwi to suit almost every garden and every gardener. These twining vines are easy to grow and tremendously satisfying, in terms of both exotic, ornamental beauty and down-to-earth, substantial nutrition.

VARIETIES

There are over 50 different species of kiwis, but they can be simply divided between two types: fuzzy and hardy. Fuzzy kiwis are the cold-tender, fairly large fruit that is seen in grocery stores. The less familiar, hardy varieties produce grape- or cherry-sized fruit with a smooth skin.

All kiwi plants love to ramble and climb, making them dramatic landscape plants as well as healthful fruit crops. The vigorous, decorative vines with their shiny green foliage and fragrant, white spring blossoms can be grown for their landscape value alone.

Fuzzy Kiwi

Fuzzy kiwi (*Actinidia deliciosa*) is a vigorous grower. Left alone under ideal growing conditions, the vines can spread out to as much as 15 feet (4 m) wide, 24 feet (7 m) long, and over 10 feet (3 m) tall. Though cold-tender, the

The fuzzy kiwi can't tolerate a deep freeze, but makes an interesting addition to gardens in more temperate climates.

vines require about 800 hours of winter chill (at 32 to 45°F [(0–7°C]). When dormant, they can survive to 10°F (–12°C). Large, deep-green leaves; white, faintly fragrant flowers; and fine red hairs covering new growth all lend an exotic air to the vines.

The fruit is oval and covered with coarse brown fuzz. The sweet/tart flavor reminds some of strawberry/pineapple, some of gooseberries. If picked while still firm, the fruit ripens and softens after harvest; it will keep refrigerated for up to six months.

HAYWARD (Zones 7 to 9) is the variety that we know from grocery stores. Fruit is up to 3 inches (8 cm) long, fuzzy skinned, with succulent, lime green flesh. The vines need about 800 hours of winter chill in order to set fruit.

SAANICHTON (Zones 7 to 9), developed in Canada, offers large, sweet, easily peeled fruit on heartily productive, somewhat more winter-hardy plants (to 5°F [–15°C]).

BLAKE (Zones 7 to 9) is a prolific variety that begins to produce fruit a year earlier than other fuzzy types and about a month earlier in the season. It fruits sparsely without a pollinator, so for a full harvest, plant a male vine nearby.

GOLDEN KIWI (Zones 7 to 9) is very similar to other fuzzy kiwifruit but is slightly less hairy; has a sweeter, less acidic flavor; and boasts striking yellow flesh.

Hardy Kiwi

Hardy kiwis (*Actinidia species*) are easy to grow, generally quite vigorous, and, as the name states, cold hardy — some extremely so. The fruits are tiny with edible skins and an interesting range of colors and tastes. Most varieties are dioecious, so require a male pollinator. (See box, next page.)

ISSAI (Zones 5–10) is the oddball of hardy kiwis. It is self-pollinating, so it can be grown as a single vine, and less vigorous, making it suitable for container growing. Its vines sport an abundance of glossy leaves throughout the season with deliciously scented white blossoms in the spring. This

Able to survive the cold better than its fuzzy cousin, the hardy kiwi offers attractive foliage and tasty fruit.

variety commonly sets fruit in the season after it is planted, a welcome contrast to those fuzzy relatives that require three to four years of subtropical weather to produce fruit. Bite-sized, 1¾-inch fruit is sweeter than that of fuzzy kiwis, but not as sweet as other hardy types. It does best in areas with a long growing season, as the fruit matures late, but is susceptible to spider mites in hot, dry climates.

ANANASNAYA or **ANANASNAJA** or just plain **Anna** (Zones 4 to 10) is a Russian introduction with a unique, pineapple flavor and striking red stems between the deep green, glossy leaves. Yields of 100 pounds per vine are not uncommon on three- to four-year-old plants. Many gardeners consider this the easiest hardy kiwi to grow.

GENEVA (Zones 5 to 9) was developed at the USDA Research Station in Geneva, New York. Its inch-long fruit is honey-sweet and ripens in September or October. Vines grow 20 to 25 feet (6–8 m).

ARCTIC BEAUTY (Zones 3 to 8) is valued for its striking deep green foliage tipped with bright pink and white. Frequently grown as an ornamental, it produces small, sweet, delicious fruit. It is an early bearer and often produces fruit the first year after planting. Plants are not as vigorous as other kiwis. Even though only the female plants produce fruit, the males of this variety boast the more dazzling display of color.

SITE AND SOIL REQUIREMENTS

Members of the kiwi family have distinct preferences when it comes to putting down roots, but once established, they provide years of beauty and bounty. Tender kiwis can be grown in the same areas as peaches and citrus; hardy varieties as far north as Zone 3.

They all tend to bloom early in the season, however, so avoid spots that are prone to late-spring frosts. A slope that facilitates cold air draining away from the plants and/or a site that allows for emergency cold-air protection is good for all.

> Kiwis contain an enzyme called actinidin. It can be used as a meat tenderizer, though some people are allergic to the substance.

Fuzzy kiwis love the easy life. Though they prefer to bask in full sun, they will produce in partial shade. They shut down in hot, dry weather, however, and are not recommended for desert areas. They need to be protected from wind, as tender new growth can snap, and they can't stand salty soil, so beachfront areas are not their favorite locales either.

What they do like is a fairly acid (pH 5 to 6.5), well-drained soil rich in organic matter and a strong trellis, fence, or other sturdy,

BOYS AND GIRLS TOGETHER

Kiwis are **dioecious,** meaning the male and female flower parts grow on separate plants. Only the female plants set fruit, and to do so they need a male pollinator nearby. They are primarily wind pollinated.

Except for the Issai, always be sure to include one male plant for every six to eight female kiwis. These are usually sold under the generic and unromantic label of "Male Pollinator."

permanent structure, such as a patio cover, for their vines.

Hardy varieties, in contrast to their fussy, fuzzy cousins, take life as it comes. Give 'em sun or give 'em shade — they will give you handfuls of yummy little kiwis. The number one requirement for these unfussy vines is that the soil be well drained. They can forgive weak soils but not wet feet.

They, too, prefer somewhat acidic soil (pH 5 to 6.5) with a healthy nitrogen balance. They cannot tolerate alkaline (high pH) or salty soils, but they do well in otherwise sandy soils. Soils rich in organic matter are best because they provide the necessary drainage and plenty of nutrients.

Like many other climbers, kiwis must have a sturdy support system to keep them off the ground and out of the rest of your garden.

Chrysanthemums or marigolds planted near kiwi vines will kill root nematodes.

PLANTING GUIDELINES

Vines are usually shipped as bare-root plants but are occasionally available potted. Because the vines are so vigorous, they are susceptible to freezes in their first season. Some growers recommend planting them in large pots and transplanting them in the garden after the danger of frost is past, to allow the young plants to establish roots and to harden somewhat over their first growing season before having to contend with cold weather.

Plant in the spring as you would any other bare-root plant (see Blackberries, page 104). After backfilling the soil, trim back the female vine to four or five healthy buds. Have winter protection handy in case of frosts.

Work about 10 pounds (4.5 kg) of compost per plant into the soil at planting time and give two doses of a good organic fertilizer each year thereafter to keep your kiwis cranking along. Feed them early in the season before the vines begin to grow and then again after the fruit has set.

Proper irrigation is critical, as kiwis often die from water-related problems. They are heavy drinkers, especially in hot weather, so keep them well watered but never soggy. The general rule of thumb is to water them daily when first transplanted, then, as the plants begin to show signs of new growth, taper off so the soil has a chance to drain between waterings.

TRAINING KIWIS TO GROW UP

Although you may get away with weak soil for kiwis, you will not get off so easily on your support system. These stout vines are vigorous and heavy; do not skimp on the building materials. Hardy kiwis also grow very quickly, so have the trellis in place at planting time.

A clothesline trellis is often recommended (see page 25). An existing pergola, carport, or other sturdy structure that can support at least two vines (remember, you'll need a separate pollinator plant for most varieties) can easily be pressed into service. Attaching heavy-gauge wire mesh to a wall also works well.

> Check periodically that the vines do not twine around the support, as twists create future weak spots in the wood.

A Three-Year Plan

Most kiwi vines are dioecious plants, meaning that for most varieties, you'll need at least one male and one female plant to set fruit. One male can pollinate six to eight female plants. A few self-fruitful varieties, such as Blake or Issai, will bear fruit with only one plant. Fruit-bearing plants require special training and pruning, similar to that of grapes, in order for the plant to produce over many years. Fortunately, all males need to do is flower, so you need only prune them to encourage new wood.

Training most varieties of kiwi vine to a trellis requires three seasons of pruning and tying. It takes this long for the trunk and lateral branches to mature enough to bear fruit.

Year One

The goal of the first season is for the female plant to grow into the overhead supports while developing strong roots. This can be accomplished by tying the main stem of the vine to a 6- to 8-foot (2–2.5 m) stake and pruning out any lateral branches that sprout from it.

Once the vine reaches the height of the overhead wires or other support — generally 6 to 7 feet (2–2.25 m) — select one shoot at the top of the vine and train it along the wire in one direction by loosely tying it in place and pruning out all others.

If the plant's trunk has not yet reached the height of the wires in the first winter, cut it down to only four to eight buds and resume training the following spring. This pruning reduces the risk of winter injury to the young plant while focusing its energy on root development.

Year Two

The following year, select another shoot and train it along the wire in the opposite direction. This allows the plant to put more energy into growing roots in the first two years than into vegetative growth.

PRUNING IS CRITICAL

A kiwi's health, appearance, and fruit production depend partly on proper pruning. Both diligent summer snipping of unproductive branches and suckers and dormant pruning of spent vines are necessary.

The basic rule for dormant pruning is to remove 60 to 70 percent of the growth in late winter or early spring. Start with branches that show signs of illness or injury, then thin out those that fruited the previous season. Finally, take out any branches that are twining around the wires or otherwise tangled. Ideally, this will leave mostly 1-year-old canes spaced about 10 to 15 inches (25–38 cm) apart for the current growing season. Most kiwifruit is produced on 1-year-old wood.

Alternatively, when the main trunk reaches the desired height, you can choose two buds to train in opposite directions along trellis wires, or up to four if you're training on a pergola or other such framework.

These vines will be the permanent arms from which all future shoots will emerge. Throughout the first season, keep an eye on the ties so that they do not constrict the swelling branches.

The second summer, your efforts will likely be rewarded with a show of fruit along the side branches that form along the horizontal arms. Tie these side branches onto the outside wires of the trellis every 24 to 30 inches (60–76 cm). Prune these canes 6 to 10 inches (15–25 cm) past the last flower bud.

During the second winter, cut off all but two or three of the side branches that bore fruit and shorten the main arms to about 5 feet (1.5 m) long.

Year Three

In the third summer, prune out any late-sprouting side branches. They shade the fruit on other branches and do not bear fruit. The final step in training comes the next winter, when the two main lateral branches should be cut back to a length of about 8 feet (2.5 m) depending on the variety; these branches are the permanent base for the sprouting side branches. Each year allow enough side branches to grow to replace those that have finished fruiting.

Male vines can be pruned hard in the summer. The goal is to maintain a nice shape and to keep them from outgrowing whatever boundaries you have set for them.

CHAPTER 17

THE ESSENTIALS OF

ESPALIER

No ancient art more successfully marries the best of form and function than espalier. The word *espalier* is a French derivative of the Italian word *spalliera* (something on which to rest the *spall*, or shoulder). It is the practice of training trees to grow in patterns along a single, flat plane. The seemingly complex process involves tying, propping, and pruning to achieve living, growing works of art and bring forth bountiful, mouthwatering harvests. Espalier is a wonderful way to satisfy your hunger for beauty as well as for delicious fruit.

Espaliered fruit trees enjoy all the same benefits as other trellised crops, including improved aeration and sunlight exposure. Manipulating the tree limbs to grow horizontally increases the number of fruiting spurs that develop and discourages nonproductive suckers from forming. Training trees to grow within a predetermined space allows you to tend and harvest trees that might otherwise get too tall to manage.

As a result of all this care, you'll enjoy more and better fruit, ease of harvest, and an elegant touch to the landscape. So while espalier may at first seem a bit fanciful, once the trees are established and producing, you'll think it's only practical. Here is a quick introduction to the beauties of this ancient art.

BASIC ESPALIER DESIGNS

The graceful form of an espaliered tree is a testament to the gardener's dedication. Although it takes only a little effort, it takes consistent effort over many years. Pruning, pinching, bending, propping, and tying must be tended to faithfully to maintain the pattern and to keep fruit production at its peak.

The design into which the tree is trained can be a formal, preconceived pattern or an informal, more free-form shape. Shaping and

Single vertical cordon

Multiple T-shape

Fan

U-shaped

Free-form

pruning, little by little, year by year, are at the heart of the gardener's art.

Formal Espalier

Trees may be trained to grow in a variety of shapes and designs depending on the artistic expression of the creative gardener and fruiting habit of the tree. Many patterns have become established as traditional because of their elegant appeal and their practicality. Here's a quick rundown of the basic shapes.

Single Vertical Cordon

The simplest example of an espaliered tree is one trained in a single arm, or cordon. It may be trained vertically, at an angle (oblique), or in a serpentine shape. Fruit trees espaliered in this fashion are often sold as "columnar trees," and are almost exclusively apple trees. A row of such trees can become a living screen or fence.

T-shaped Design

Two horizontal cordons trained in opposite directions create a T-shaped tree. This shape can be expanded over time to create multiple horizontal arms on as many levels as desired. Or multiple vertical arms from two horizontal cordons can be trained to form a gridiron design.

U-shaped Design

Two vertical cordons trained into a horizontal base can be further trained to form a U-shape, which can be further expanded into double or triple U's. A design featuring U's within U's, called the Palmette Verrier, looks like a candelabra.

V-shaped Design

This design lends itself to a number of variations. Several V's planted in a row so they crisscross is called a Belgian fence. Add one or more side arms to each tree in a 45-degree angle to grow a Losange. The V's may also be continued upward into a Palmette Oblique pattern, a single vertical trunk with V's centered along the middle.

Arcure Design

An Arcure espalier produces an elegant, interlocking design of arches upon arches.

CHOOSING THE RIGHT SPOT

It's common to see trees espaliered along walls, buildings, and fences in order to maximize the use of ground space. A south-facing wall will increase heat retention — absorbing heat during the day and releasing it at night, as well as heating up earlier in the spring and retaining that heat later into the fall — over open planting areas. This can work for you in cool-climate areas or against you in hot ones.

Another common site for a row of espaliered trees is alongside a driveway or property line. Before planting in this situation, consider road pollutants, traffic compaction of the soil, and which side of the trees will bear fruit — your side or your neighbor's! Try to position the row so that it runs north to south. Fruit-bearing spurs tend to form facing the light. An east-to-west wall of trees will produce almost all of its fruit on the south side — something to remember if you are planning a property divider with a southerly neighbor.

Informal Espalier

Informal designs work well for trees that fruit on the previous season's growth, such as cherries and plums, because they allow for new shoots to be worked in every year.

Fan Design

A fan is a design in which several cordons rise from a low trunk and are trained to grow up and out at different angles.

Free-form Designs

These designs tend to emerge as a tree grows and offers up buds in random places. As new wood develops each year, the gardener can retain the best-placed, healthiest buds wherever they sprout.

No garden need go without the sweet scent and elegant beauty of flowering fruit trees or the rich rewards of their harvest. Even the most limited garden, patio, or balcony can provide room for one or two espaliered fruit trees.

> When buying trees, specify that you plan to espalier and ask for recommendations that will suit your growing conditions, your preferred fruiting variety, and your plans.

CHOOSING THE RIGHT TREES

The best trees to espalier are usually dwarf or semidwarf types because they have been bred to occupy a small space, but be aware that the process of espalier training dwarfs tree growth even more. Dwarf-tree trunks and limbs won't grow as thick as those of a standard fruit tree, and even without training, they don't grow nearly as tall (30 feet [9 m] or more!). These smaller trees may be genetically dwarfed — some are so small they are called miniatures — or standard varieties that have been grafted onto dwarf rootstock.

The roots determine more than just the size of the tree, so be particular about the rootstock you choose. Rootstock varieties differ almost as much as fruiting varieties, each with its own idiosyncrasies. Some are drought resistant; some are not. Some tolerate poor soils or other adverse growing conditions better than others.

You may be able to find trees that have already been started in an espalier pattern, but if you have to start at the very beginning, choose bare-root plants or one- or two-year-old whips. They have the best chance of survival, generally bear fruit earlier than transplanted potted trees, are the easiest to train, and are the cheapest to buy.

ALL SORTS OF APPLES

Approximately 7,500 different varieties of apples (*Malus* spp.) exist, with about 2,500 grown in the United States — in an array of tastes, textures, colors, ripening times, and more. So how does one choose?

Some apple varieties are more suited to home gardens than others, primarily because many are so prone to diseases that you would need heavy pesticide regimens to get a decent crop. So your first step is to look for disease-resistant varieties, such as Pristine, Yellow Transparent, Freedom, Liberty, Jonafree, Enterprise, and Goldrush.

Climate requirements are critical. Your climate zone must agree with a tree's cold tolerance, heat tolerance, and winter-chill requirements. Since most apple trees require significant winter chill (dormancy at temperatures from 32 to 45°F [0–7°C]), they do better in the North, but not too far north. Early-blooming varieties that are otherwise cold hardy can lose entire crops to a spring frost.

> For formal espalier, avoid tip-bearing varieties that naturally form clusters of fruit at the end of long shoots. Their fruiting habit makes it next to impossible to maintain a formal design and still get a harvest.

Climate-adapted varieties tolerate temperature extremes that often discourage other types. Some exceptionally cold-hardy varieties (hardy down to Zone 3: –40 to –30°F [–40 to –34°C]) are Yellow Transparent, Norland, Prairie Spy, Haralred, Honeycrisp, and Honeygold. Of course, the opposite problem, insufficient winter chill, can be a problem to southern gardeners.

Some varieties with low chill requirements are Dorsett Golden (requires as few as 100 chill hours), Tropic Sweet (150 chill hours), Anna (150 to 300 chill hours), Pink Lady or Cripps Pink (200 to 400 chill hours), and Winter Banana (300 to 400 chill hours).

Varieties

Since most apples must cross-pollinate, you'll need to select at least two different varieties with compatible flowering/ripening times. Most pros recommend early-ripening fruit for home growing because those varieties are least likely to suffer from fungal diseases and other problems that come on toward the end of the growing season.

The downside, though, is that the fruit of most early-fruiting (i.e., summer-bearing) varieties, doesn't hold up well in storage. The best keep about month. The answer for many gardeners may be to try to fit in one or two varieties of staggered ripening times to extend the harvests and reap the benefits of the different types.

Some recommendations are early ripeners like these:

LODI (Zones 4–8) ripens in July, producing green, crisp, tart fruit that is excellent for cooking.

PRISTINE (Zones 4–9) produces yellow, mildly tart fruit that is good fresh, baked, or sauced. Highly resistant to scab and cedar apple rust, somewhat to powdery mildew and fire blight.

REDFREE (Zones 5–8) is highly resistant to apple scab and cedar apple rust, with good resistance to fire blight and mildew. The fruit is red and sweet.

YELLOW TRANSPARENT (Zones 3–8) produces yellow, crisp, sweet fruit that ripens earlier than other apples. These are disease-resistant, cold-hardy, and long-lived trees.

Midseason varieties to try include the following:

CORTLAND (Zones 4–6) ripens mid-September. Fruit is red with white flesh that resists browning, best for pies and cider.

EMPIRE (Zones 4–7) produces red fruit that ripens in mid-September. Trees resist fire blight and rust.

GOLDRUSH (Zones 5–8) apples are yellow, crisp, and tart, excellent fresh or baked. Highly resistant to apple scab and powdery mildew.

GRAVENSTEIN (Zones 4–9) ripens early September. The crisp, tangy fruit is yellow tinged with red. Trees are biennial bearers, offering good crops in alternate years.

HONEYCRISP (Zones 3–6) is exceptionally cold hardy. Red, sweet, crisp fruit ripens late midseason and is excellent for both eating fresh and keeping.

LIBERTY (Zones 4–9) has dark red, sweet/tart apples on trees that are very resistant to scab and mildew.

Later ripeners like these have the advantage of keeping up to six months when refrigerated or root-cellared:

ENTERPRISE (Zones 4–7) ripens mid- to late-season, producing red, firm, crisp apples that are mildly tart. Extreme resistance to apple scab, cedar apple rust, and fire blight; some resistance to powdery mildew. Fruit keeps 5 to 6 months when refrigerated.

GOLDEN DELICIOUS (Zones 4–8) ripens in October; fruit is yellow, sweet, and crisp.

HALARED (Zones 3–7) ripens mid- to late-season. The red, firm, sweet apples keep well, and the trees have some resistance to fire blight. It is exceptionally cold hardy.

PRAIRIE SPY (Zones 3–9) trees bear young. The large, yellow-washed-with-red fruit ripens late. Apples are crisp and juicy with excellent flavor; they keep well in storage for several months.

If you absolutely have room for only one tree, then your choices are limited a self-fertile variety. Self-fertile varieties will set fruit, some more reliably than others, with no pollination from a second tree. They are perfect for that truly tiny garden space.

DORSETT GOLDEN (Zones 5–8) requires as few as 100 hours of winter chill. Yellow fruit ripens early, resembles Golden Delicious.

JONARED (Zones 5–8) produces bright red, sweet/tart apples that ripen in mid-September. A good all-purpose apple.

NEWTOWN PIPPIN (Zones 4–9) ripens late season, producing a green, tart, crisp, all-purpose apple.

QUEEN COX (Zones 4–9) ripens in early September. Disease-resistant trees grow delicious apples that are yellow with some red. *This is the only truly reliable self-fertile apple for most home gardens.*

Apple Tree Basics

Apples are the darlings of espalier gardeners for good reason. They offer an astounding variety of tempting fruit, and their growth habit allows them to bear for years within the confines of an espalier design. They can successfully be trained to almost any design, but yields are highest when branches are trained to a 45-degree angle.

A well-tended apple tree can produce for 50 years, beginning in its second or third season. All that it requires is minimum attention to its basic needs. Adequate water is one fundamental requirement.

Pollination is another basic need; without it, the apple tree won't produce fruit. Most varieties are self-sterile (meaning that they require a tree of another variety to provide pollen) or, at best, partially self-pollinating. The pollinator variety must flower at the same time as the fruiting variety and provide adequate amounts of pollen. Check with your tree supplier about which varieties will cross-pollinate with those you want to espalier.

PLUMP, PERFECT PEARS

Closely related to apples, pears are the next best choice for espaliered fruit trees, a fact that contributed greatly to their rise in popularity in Europe. Domesticated by the early Romans and Phoenicians, pears eventually became prized by French nobility.

Most pears need a pollinator variety nearby to produce fruit. Starking Delicious (also called Maxine) is a good-tasting, disease-resistant pear that is available in dwarf form and acts as a pollinator for many other varieties.

The problem was that Paris didn't have the best growing conditions for the fruit. By espaliering the trees, growers were able to facilitate ripening, and the persnickety pear became the fruit du jour.

Varieties

Pears were introduced to North America in 1629 by the Massachusetts Company when it imported seeds from England. Today, there are some 5,000 varieties known worldwide.

The two most common kinds of pears (*Pyrus* spp.) grown in North America are European pears and Asian pears. European pears, such as Bartlett, the most commonly grown pear in the world, are the most familiar. They define the classic pear shape, whereas Asian pears are more apple-shaped.

Pears come in a surprising array of tastes, textures, colors, and even shapes. They can be classified as sweet, spicy, or tart with varying degrees of intensity. They may have firm, soft, juicy, dry, or grainy flesh, and come in skin colors from yellow and green to cinnamon brown and deep red, with or without speckles and/or blushes (called cheek or russet). Some are small, some are large; some are classically pear-shaped, some are squatty; and some are just plain round.

As with apple varieties, pears can be early-, mid-, or late-season bearers; are generally not self-fruitful; and display varying degrees of cold tolerance and disease resistance. They can also be grafted onto a variety of rootstocks that affect their growth and performance. Clearly, choosing a pear tree to grow goes well beyond the familiar!

European Pears

European pears (*P. communis*) may be short and sweet or elongated and spicy, but all are at least somewhat pear shaped. The flesh is usually fine and buttery, making these the preferred dessert-quality fruit for eating out of hand. Most varieties are very susceptible to fire blight, so much so that growing them in areas where fire blight is a problem — regions with a warm, humid spring, such as the southern East Coast and the Southeast — is discouraged. Some good choices for espalier are noted below.

BARTLETT, also known as **WILLIAMS' BON CHRÉTIEN** (Zones 5–9), is the pear known around the world for its fresh-eating and canning quality. Fruit ripens in late August. Picked light green, it matures to warm yellow; the sweet and juicy fruit keeps well.

Trees are productive with a compact habit, but rather susceptible to diseases. **RED BARTLETT** produces red-skinned fruit.

BOSC (Zones 4–9) is an exceptionally fragrant pear with a slender, elongated shape, cinnamon brown color, dense/crisp texture, and a spicy/sweet flavor. The fruit ripens in mid-September and keeps very well. Somewhat self-fertile, it is a favorite among home growers.

CLAPP'S FAVORITE (Zones 4–8) ripens in mid-August. Very cold-hardy, productive trees produce juicy, melting, fine-fleshed fruit that keeps only about six weeks. **RED CLAPP**, also known as **KALLE**, is deep red and fine fleshed, considered by many the best of red pears, and strikingly attractive in espalier.

COMICE (Zones 5–9) is the pear shipped in gourmet gift boxes. Squatty greenish yellow fruits are the sweetest and juiciest of all pears, with a texture often described as creamy. Ripens in August. Self-fertile in the West, it has a low chill requirement of only 200–300 hours, and is somewhat fire blight resistant.

D'ANJOU (Zones 4–9) is among the very juiciest of pears with excellent dessert quality. The large, fat-bottomed fruit in light green to maroon (it doesn't change color as it ripens) ripens mid-September.

MOONGLOW (Zones 5–9) ripens late August to September, producing dessert-quality, medium to large pears with red-blushed yellow skin and nearly gritless flesh. Trees are very productive, starting early in life, and highly resistant to fire blight.

POTOMAC (Zones 5–8) is a cross between Moonglow and D'Anjou that ripens in early September. It has fine, sweet, buttery flesh like D'Anjou, but the fruit is small. The moderately vigorous tree is highly resistant to fire blight. Fruit keeps 8 to 10 weeks.

RESCUE (Zones 5–9) ripens in September. The brilliant red-orange fruit is sweet, smooth, and juicy, with a small core. Tree is scab resistant, vigorous, and productive.

SECKEL (Zones 4–9), also called the sugar pear, is the smallest pear grown. Even the trees are naturally dwarf. The dessert-quality fruit, which ripens in late August, matures to a deep wine red, is aromatic, and tastes delectably sweet and spicy. Self-fertile in warm areas, but needs a pollinator in colder climes. Adapted to a wide range of growing conditions, it is resistant to fire blight but susceptible to scab.

WARREN (Zones 5–8) is extremely resistant to fire blight. Medium to large fruit have excellent dessert-type flavor and quality with a fine, smooth, buttery, grit-free texture. Skin is greenish with a bronze wash; ripens in August.

As with apple trees, avoid tip-bearing varieties such as Jargonelle, Josephine de Malines, and Packham's Triumph, as they won't produce fruit in formal espalier patterns.

Asian Pears

Asian pears (*P. pyrifolia*), also called apple-pears or pear-apples, have a mild pear flavor, with a crisp texture and a round shape more similar to an apple than to a European pear. They are very juicy but can be bland tasting. Most varieties are prone to fire blight. Some popular varieties are noted on the next page.

HOSUI (Zones 5–8) fruit has a higher acid content than many Asian pears for a more tart taste. Trees bloom late (avoiding spring frosts), bear fruit in August, and are moderately resistant to fire blight. They are self-pollinating, though will bear more fruit with pollination.

KOSUI (Zones 6–9) is not suitable for wet climates, as it is susceptible to pseudomonas. Russet-colored, medium to large fruit ripens August and is better tasting than most.

OLYMPIC, also called **KOREAN GIANT** and **DAN BAE** (Zones 5–9), is very vigorous, bearing young and heavily. Trees flower early in the season and fruit ripens mid-October. The green fruit is large, crisp, and juicy, and stores for five months.

Pear juice is often recommended for babies and the ill. It is said to reduce fever, improve immunity, reduce inflammation, clear phlegm, and soothe a sore throat.

SHINKO (Zones 6–9) is the most fire-blight-resistant Asian pear. Fruit is bronze over green, with firm, smooth, sweet, distinctively flavored, juicy flesh. Ripens late August and keeps well.

SHINSEIKI (Zones 3–11) bears medium-sized, good dessert-quality, yellow-skinned, speckled fruit. Ripens July to August. Easy to grow, self-fruitful with moderate fire blight resistance.

20TH CENTURY, also called **NIJISSEIKI**, (Zones 5–9) ripens July to August and produces dessert-quality, medium-sized yellow fruit that keeps well. The small, heavily bearing trees are easy to grow and moderately fire blight resistant.

YOINASHI (Zones 5–9) bears fruit in late September. Round, brown, crisp, and juicy fruit tastes like butterscotch when ripe. Trees are vigorous, very productive, and pseudomonas resistant.

Pear Tree Basics

Pear trees generally live even longer than apple trees, and a happy one can easily bear for decades. Pick a spot it loves, and that old pear tree could well become your legacy. Those on my family's homestead orchard are about 100 years old and still producing flush crops every other year.

Pears are choosier about climate and soil than almost any other fruit tree. They are less cold tolerant than apples but less heat tolerant than peaches. They thrive in damp, overcast regions like the coastal Pacific Northwest but are doomed to blight in warm humidity. Pears do best in acid soil (common in damp areas), with a pH of 6.0 to 6.5 being ideal, but they will perform well within the 5.0 to 7.5 pH range.

Avoid planting in low-lying areas, as they collect frosts. Pears are early-season bloomers, and lingering frosts can damage or destroy blossoms, severely hampering yields. Cold-air sinks can also damage buds, new shoots, and prolong ripening times. Look for a sloping site that sweeps cold air downwind. The dwarf varieties on quince roots are shallow rooted, which makes them more susceptible to extreme summer heat and deep frosts.

Pears prefer fertile soil, which makes most gardens a perfect site. They can tolerate poorer drainage than most other fruit trees and do well in heavy loam clay. In fact, pears abhor the light loam and gravelly soils that apples adore. If forced to grow in dry soil, the tree will retaliate by producing bitter, gritty fruit.

Training Pears to Grow Up

Like apples, pears bear fruit on long-lived spurs that lend themselves well to formal espalier. They can be finicky trees to grow and often get into the habit of biennial bearing, which produces a bumper crop one year and little to nothing the next. But their delicate blossoms and sumptuous fruit make them worth any peculiarities that they may exhibit.

Because their fruiting habit is the same, pears are just as versatile in espalier designs as are apples. However, unlike apples, pears tend to fruit more on vertical cordons than horizontal or angular ones, so designs that incorporate vertical cordons will provide the highest fruit production. Gridiron, Palmette Oblique, and U designs are all well suited to pears.

APRICOTS, PEACHES, AND NECTARINES

Gardeners often shy away from apricots, peaches, and nectarines because the larger stone fruits have acquired persnickety reputations. They do require more attention than other fruit trees in terms of pruning, frost protection, and pest and disease control, but the spectacular displays of limb-smothering blossoms and generous offerings of delectable, sun-ripened fruit make up for the extra effort. With a little special treatment, an espaliered apricot, peach, or nectarine tree will do you proud.

Varieties

Apricots, peaches, and nectarines are not as naturally suited to espalier as are apples and pears. Most are not especially cold hardy. However, with careful attention to fruiting habits, they can still be coaxed into producing a luscious harvest. The following varieties are reliable, adaptable to a variety of climates, and easy to find on the market.

Apricots

There are a few distinctions to be made with apricots. Some are larger than others, some produce fruit earlier, and some are more cold resistant, although all are hardier than peaches and nectarines. There are also some differences in pollination requirements. Here are few good choices:

Peaches and nectarines begin to produce their juicy, golden treasures during their second season and are in full swing by the fourth or fifth year. Apricots may lag a year behind.

BLENHEIM (Zones 6–9) produces medium to large fruit with thick, sweet, extremely juicy, yellowish flesh (the classic California apricot) early to midseason.

FLORAGOLD (Zones 7–9) bears small to medium fruits in midseason. This genetic dwarf grows only 6 to 8 feet (2–2.5 m) tall and bears an early, heavy crop.

GOLDCOT (Zones 4–8) is a medium to large, mid- to late-season fruit with a sweet flavor that stands up to processing or fresh eating. It is hardy and self-pollinating, a necessity for the gardener who has room for only one tree.

HARCOT (Zones 5–9) is a medium-sized, firm, sweet, juicy early apricot.

MOORPARK (Zones 6–9) has been a midseason favorite since the 1700s with juicy, aromatic flesh and sweet rich flavor.

ROYALTY (Zones 7–9) is an early harvest variety with large fruit.

Peaches

There are over 2,000 varieties of peaches with a range of colors, ripening times, hardiness, chill requirements, and resistance to disease, but they all produce round, fuzzy, melt-in-your-mouth fruit. Some are freestone (the pit removes easily); some are clingstone (it hangs on for dear life). The following are just a few examples:

ELBERTA (Zones 5–8). Long the gold standard, this late season variety produces large, round, golden fruit with a red blush. It adapts well to a range of soils and temperate climates.

EMPRESS (Zones 5–8) grows quickly to about 5 feet tall and produces large, deliciously sweet, glowing red-pink clingstone fruit. It is the most cold hardy dwarf variety. It requires about 850 hours of winter chill.

GARDEN GOLD (Zones 6–9) is a vigorously growing variety, reaching 5 to 6 feet in height. It flowers a week later than most varieties, so is less vulnerable to frost, and even does well in poor soils. The freestone fruit is soft with a good, melting flavor.

HONEY BABE (Zones 6–8) grows 4 to 6 feet tall, producing sweet, firm, medium-sized freestone fruit. It requires about 500 hours of winter chill.

REDHAVEN (Zones 5–7) is another adaptable peach with firm, deep, red skin and yellow flesh that doesn't brown when exposed to air.

Nectarines

Nectarines vary somewhat in appearance, but the rich aroma and melting, peachlike flavor are unmistakable. With only one recessive gene to set them apart, nectarines are really just bald peaches. They vary in ripening times, hardiness, and disease resistance.

DESERT DAWN (Zones 7–9) and **JUNEGLO** (Zones 6–7) are exceptionally flavorful varieties that both ripen early.

FANTASIA (Zones 5–9) and **RUBYGRAND** (Zones 6–9) are large-fruited mid- to late-season varieties with red flesh and superb flavor.

MERICREST (Zones 5–8), which ripens in mid-season, is very cold hardy and offers some disease resistance.

Stone Fruit Basics

The fact that 95 percent of the apricots and 90 percent of the peaches and nectarines grown in the United States are grown in California tells us a little about their preferences.

Like other fruit trees, apricots, peaches, and nectarines benefit from the air and water drainage that accompany a slope. They demand good drainage and a soil that will hold warmth. Rocky, gravelly, or sandy soils are ideal. Clay and loam, if well drained and deep, will be politely tolerated by peaches and nectarines, but apricots do best in a deep, sandy loam.

The soil, however, does not have to be especially fertile. These trees draw heavily on potassium, calcium, and magnesium, but too much nitrogen prompts lots of vegetation that often gets caught by frost before it matures.

If you live in a good peach-growing area, you usually cannot make a mistake when you decide where to place your tree. If you are not in such an area, you should remember that the foremost need of a peach tree is warmth. They are temperamental trees that demand a sufficient winter chill and a warm summer.

Low spots, corners, and flat sites may collect cold, still air that threatens the trees with freezing in the winter or frost damage during flowering. In colder climates, some type of shelter, such as that afforded by espaliering along a wall or fence, is greatly appreciated.

Training Stone Fruits to Grow Up

Apricots, peaches, and nectarines bear fruit on one-year-old wood. Once a portion of a limb has set fruit, it is finished for the life of the tree. In a naturally shaped tree, this keeps the fruit developing on the outside of the tree, where it receives the most light. In order to keep new wood coming, heavy pruning is a necessity.

Unfortunately, this fact limits the espalier design to either an informal shape or a fan. The espalier will amply reward your efforts due to the openness of the tree and the constant summer pinching, pruning, and attention that all promote good health and great harvests.

PLEASING PLUMS

Virtually every garden in the continental United States can successfully grow some type of plum. There are 2,000 or so types of plums, divided into several groups. The most commonly grown plum trees in North America are the (mostly) self-pollinating European, followed by cross-pollinating Japanese types. Native plums and hybrids fill in the gaps where other types won't grow.

European Plums

European plums run the gamut of shape, size, color, flavor, and texture. They include egg-shaped, dark blue-violet varieties, such as the prune plums, which develop thick, sweet flesh perfect for drying.

DAMSON (Zones 5–9) produces small, dark purple, oval-shaped fruit with golden, spicy/tart flesh. Hardy, pest-resistant trees tolerate some shade and thrive where others waiver.

EARLY LAXTON (Zones 5–9) produces delicious, pinkish orange, freestone fruit early in the season. It needs a pollinator. The fruit is especially high in vitamin C.

ITALIAN PRUNE, also known as **Fellenburg,** (Zones 5 to 9) produces sweet, deep purple, medium-sized fruit that is exceptional fresh, canned, or dried into prunes. Trees bloom late in the spring, which makes them a great choice for areas with late frosts or a cool, wet spring.

KUBAN DELIGHT (Zones 5–9) is very productive, offering loads of small, round, juicy, sweet-fleshed fruit with tart reddish purple skin on disease-resistant trees.

Plum trees begin bearing in their third year and continue bearing for nearly 20 more. The fruit tends to ripen in waves rather than all at once.

MIRABELLE DE METZ (Zones 4–9) is an old French cultivar. This deep yellow plum boasts superb sweet flavor.

STANLEY (Zones 4–9) is an old favorite for its dependable production of sweet, juicy, deep purple fruit. Flesh is firm, orange-tinged, and very high in sugar content, making it delectable fresh and ideal for drying. Blooms late and produces without a pollinator.

VICTORIA (Zones 5–9) plums are beloved for their profusion of large, ovoid, pinkish fruit with gold/yellow, sweet, freestone flesh that is excellent for canning

Japanese Plums

Japanese plums produce large round fruits in a variety of colors. They bloom earlier in the spring than do Europeans, which makes them susceptible to spring frosts. Most plums are dwarfed by grafting onto apricot, Nanking cherry, or native rootstocks. Although plum trees do not reach the grand sizes of some other fruit trees, it is still a good idea to request dwarf stock when you are planning to espalier plum trees.

Many varieties are native to the United States and prosper in their particular regions. There are also some that have been bred for special areas.

BURBANK (Zones 5–9) produces ultra-sweet, purple/red, semi-freestone fruit on a naturally semidwarf tree.

EMBER (Zone 3) is from Maine, so it has to be cold hardy. Medium-sized, red round fruit has firm, meaty, sweet flesh great for cooking or eating fresh.

PIPESTONE (Zones 4–8) offers loads of red plums with tough, easily peeled skin and juicy, sweet, golden flesh.

REDHEART (Zones 5–9) has sweet, fine, bright red flesh with deep red skin. Great for jams and preserves.

SANTA ROSA (Zones 5–9) produces gorgeous large, sweet red fruit with golden-colored flesh on vigorous, easy to grow trees.

SATSUMA (Zones 5–9) produces dark red fruit with deep, firm, juicy red flesh.

SHIRO (Zones 4–9) grows large round, yellow, divinely sweet and juicy plums on very productive trees.

UNDERWOOD (Zone 3) plums have yellow, freestone flesh that is sweet and juicy, grown on dependably productive, vigorous trees with a longer than usual harvest season.

Plum Tree Basics

Regional climate is the first limiting factor of which type of plum to plant. European plums prosper in most temperate areas, as they tolerate cold fairly well and require a certain amount of winter chill to set fruit.

Japanese plums are more cold sensitive but handle summer heat better than do the European types. Japanese plums thrive in the same areas as peaches do.

Like peaches, plums perform best in a slightly protected area or on a gentle slope. A north-facing slope is often recommended for northern growers because the cooler spring air may help to delay the early blooming that is so susceptible to frost.

Soil preferences vary with the type of plum tree: European plums favor clay; Damson plums revel in the heaviest soils. Almost any type of soil with good drainage can support some type of plum tree.

Training Plums to Grow Up

Unfortunately, neither European nor Japanese plums are particularly well suited to espalier because of their fruit-bearing habits. Japanese plums generally fruit on spurs that grow on new wood, whereas most of the other varieties bear on short-lived spurs and shoots that grow on older wood. Japanese plums tend to send up many vertical branches and so will bear best in designs that incorporate vertical, or near vertical, cordons.

Informal espalier and fan shapes are the easiest to maintain. Vertical cordon patterns, such as Palmette Oblique, U designs, and the Gridiron, are also appropriate for plums, but may prove more challenging to keep fruiting.

Except for the Japanese varieties, plum trees do not often require fruit thinning. Given the larger-sized plum that they produce, Japanese plums, however, should be thinned to a spacing of 4 to 6 inches (10–15 cm) between the developing fruit. This not only produces larger, almost perfect plums, but also reduces the risk of overloaded branches breaking from excess weight.

APPENDIX 1

A NOTE ON RECOMMENDED

VARIETIES

Recommending specific varieties for all gardeners is a crap shoot at best. Differences in climate, soil, and gardener preferences make it even iffier. Add the fact that by the time this book goes to print, there could be dozens of new cultivars hitting the market, and you can see the scope of such an endeavor.

But some varieties are just better suited to growing vertically than others, so I've listed those that have prospered either for me personally or for well-established sources. Rarely do I rely on marketing material, gathering most of my data from independent testers and university comparisons.

The cultivars were chosen with these criteria in mind:

★ Wide range of growing conditions and climates
★ Ease of growing
★ Availability (which is a killer because some really great varieties, both new and old, are hard to find)
★ Suitability to growing vertically
★ Excellent eating quality/flavor
★ Disease resistance

If you don't see a variety you prefer listed, it might be that it isn't as cold tolerant as another variety, thereby limiting where it can be grown, or perhaps it has a penchant for root rot that drops it out of the front runners. Or I ran out of space. Or I just haven't discovered it yet!

If you are curious about a specific cultivar, compare notes with other gardeners who share their experiences and reviews online or at local garden clubs. Visiting your local nursery or county Extension agent puts you face-to-face with the folks who know the very best varieties for your neck of the woods.

Key to Variety Listings

On the next page, you'll find a quick primer of abbreviations and terms used in the recommendations.

AAS WINNER. All American Selection Winner. Look for this as a sure sign that the variety will grow in a wide range of areas. These varieties have proved outstanding in extensive test trials throughout the United States.

GY (GYNOECIOUS). Plants that produce only female (fruiting) flowers.

HYBRID. You can expect improved performance all around for this type of plant. What you cannot expect, however, is to save and plant the seeds and get a repeat performance. Hybrids are the product of two different strains, and while generally more vigorous than either parent, their seed is either sterile or produces unpredictable, or inferior, plants.

MO (MONECIOUS). Plants that produce both male and female flowers on the same plant.

OP (OPEN-POLLINATED). This means that the seeds from this variety can be saved and planted to yield a whole new crop just like the crop it was saved from (providing it hasn't been cross-pollinated).

PATENTED. These varieties cannot legally be propagated until their patent expires. Also seen in catalogs as Plant Patent and PPAF (Plant Patent Applied For) when patent pending. Once a patent expires, it is usually fine to propagate the plant freely. U.S. plant patents filed before June 8, 1995, expire 17 years from the date of filing (or in some cases 20 years); plant patents filed after June 8, 1995, expire 20 years from the date of issue.

X NUMBER OF DAYS, SUCH AS 85 DAYS. This refers to the average number of days between planting and harvesting. Some plants ripen all at once; others begin to yield around this time and then continue to produce for an extended harvest.

But remember it's an average. Individual circumstances will affect the number of days until your crop passes from your vines to your lips. Also, know that different sources often report different numbers of days to harvest for the same crop.

ZONES, SUCH AS ZONES 5–9. This refers to cold-hardiness zones as described by the United States Department of Agriculture (USDA). It is important to know your zone for perennial plants because selecting plants that are insufficiently cold hardy means essentially signing their death warrant when you write the check. A plant listed as hardy to a specific zone has proved to survive down to a certain cold temperature.

It is not a guarantee, but a guideline. Anything that stresses a plant — such as drought, disease or nutrient deficiency — can weaken its cold hardiness. Experts recommend choosing plants hardy to one zone colder than the zone in which you live, as unexpected cold snaps are bound to happen.

USDA HARDINESS ZONE MAP

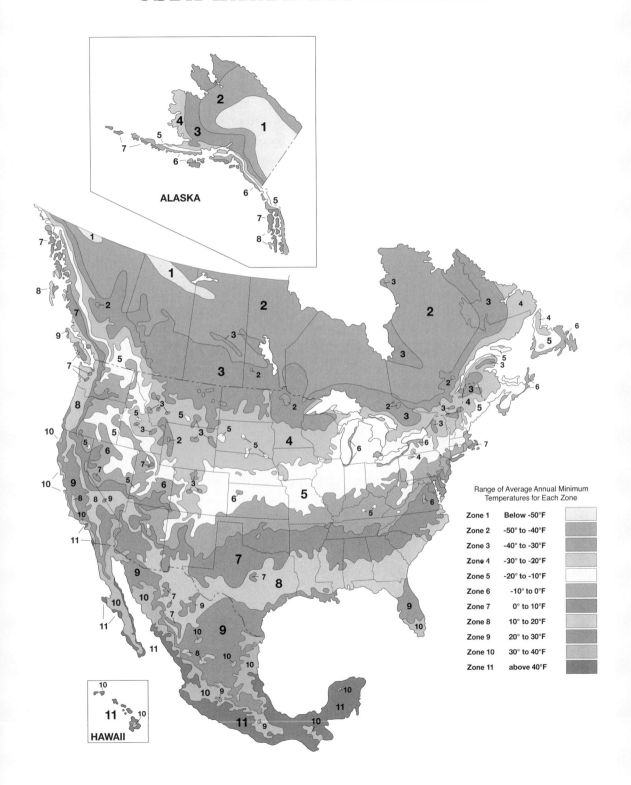

Range of Average Annual Minimum
Temperatures for Each Zone

Zone 1	Below -50°F
Zone 2	-50° to -40°F
Zone 3	-40° to -30°F
Zone 4	-30° to -20°F
Zone 5	-20° to -10°F
Zone 6	-10° to 0°F
Zone 7	0° to 10°F
Zone 8	10° to 20°F
Zone 9	20° to 30°F
Zone 10	30° to 40°F
Zone 11	above 40°F

ALASKA

HAWAII

APPENDIX 2

DIRECT SEEDING

Most garden vegetables — even tomatoes — can be sown directly into the garden. Of course, this works only in areas with a growing season long enough for the plants to fruit. (For ways to extend a moderate growing season, see below.)

Among the benefits of direct seeding is bypassing all of those steps of providing the appropriate heat and light, hardening off the seedlings, and transplanting them successfully. Directly seeded plants grow stronger from the start than do their coddled counterparts, and can grow to equal the transplants or even surpass them in size and productivity.

The main disadvantage is that crops can take longer to mature without the head start afforded by transplanting. Direct seeding also takes up valuable ground space for a longer period of time as the plants mature, which can be a problem if you want to plant certain successive crops in a single season (e.g. if you have a bed full of baby squash plants in place, you can't sow an early spinach crop there and put in the squash seedlings a few weeks later).

Follow seed packet instructions for soil depth and spacing and the best time of year to plant for your area. Although most garden seeds usually germinate in 5 to 12 days at 70 to 75° F (21–24° C), cool soil slows their emergence. You can speed things up a bit by prewarming the soil.

One of the easiest ways to do this is to cover the prepared seedbed with plastic sheeting two weeks prior to planting and leave it there, held in place with stakes or weights. Black plastic absorbs more heat, but clear radiates it more efficiently into the soil. You should be able to tell by feel after a few days that the soil beneath the plastic is noticeably warmer than the surrounding soil, but if you want to know exactly how much warmer, use a soil thermometer.

When ready to plant, peel back the sheet. Sow your seeds, then put it back in place when you're done. Keep the soil covered until the seeds sprout. As the seedlings grow, leave the plastic loosely in place to protect them from frosts. Remove plastic to water, and when temperatures rise during the day.

Take it off for good as soon as night temperatures stay above 50° F (10° C). After the third set of leaves appears on the seedlings, thin to the appropriate spacing for each type of plant by snipping off the ones you don't want at ground level.

APPENDIX 3

GROWING YOUR OWN
SEEDLINGS

You can start transplants either indoors in containers or outside in a cold frame to get a jump on the growing season. It's a good idea if you have a short growing season, and for plants such as tomatoes and peppers that originated in the tropics and require a long, warm season. Giving your plants an early start will allow them to begin producing earlier, giving you a much better return for your gardening investment.

Always start in pots made of peat or other biodegradable material, and transplant them pot and all to avoid disturbing roots. Some veggies that are best started in containers are:

★ Broccoli
★ Cantaloupe
★ Cauliflower
★ Lettuces
★ Peppers
★ Tomatoes

Seed-Starting Supplies

The only requirements for transplant containers is that they must be at least 2½ inches deep to allow for young, spreading roots, and they must have drainage holes. Those nicely matching plastic models at the garden center are a landfill nightmare. If you must buy them, use them carefully, wash them thoroughly, and *reuse* them.

The possibilities for free containers are endless! For starters, almost any food-safe container will do. Look around the house, garage, and workshop for other ideas. Here are a few to start your imagination going:

★ Cut milk cartons lengthwise and slice a few holes in the bottom for drainage.
★ Large, wax-coated cereal boxes and Styrofoam take-out containers are made-to-order seed starters.
★ For a built-in greenhouse effect, save clear plastic boxes from delis and bakeries. Poke holes in the bottom, fill with potting soil, plant, and put the lids on.
★ Wash out used margarine or yogurt cups and plastic trays from snack foods.
★ Save toilet paper rolls, cut them in half widthwise, arrange on a tray, and fill.
★ Piece together wooden flats from scrap lumber, but don't use old painted wood or

treated lumber, as it may contain toxins that could leach into the container soil.

★ Scrounge up trays to place beneath the draining containers. A shallow box lined with plastic wrap or a cookie tray will work in a pinch.

★ Save plastic lids to put under larger pots.

Temperature and Light Requirements

Temperature is critical to how many seeds germinate and develop. Room temperature, 65 to 70°F (18.3–21.1°C), works well to germinate most seeds, although some require higher or lower temperatures. Check seed packets, catalogs, or a good online source (see Resources) for specifics.

A gentle heat source underneath the seed containers encourages roots to grow downward. Once plants sprout, however, remove the bottom heat, as cooler temperatures produce sturdier plants.

Seedlings need a balance of light and warmth to grow. Too much light and not enough heat and they may not grow at all. Start with lights on for 16 hours a day, no more than 12 inches above the seedlings, and gradually decrease to 12 hours.

Too much heat and not enough light causes them to grow pale and spindly. Plants grown on a windowsill will do fine if the microclimate near the window is cool enough — just be sure to turn them regularly or they will bend toward the source of light.

You don't need a full-spectrum grow-light for anything unless it has to flower and set fruit, so most seedlings do fine with just the cool range found in normal fluorescents.

The alternative is to purchase cool-watt fluorescent lights. Sold as shop lights in 4- and 8-foot lengths, the lights are inexpensive and perfectly adequate for seed starting. Hang them within a few inches of the plants' tops, and adjust the height of the lights as the seedlings grow.

APPENDIX 4

HARDENING OFF
TENDER TRANSPLANTS

The most critical step to take before setting out transplants is to harden them off. They've grown in a protected environment thus far, with mild temperatures, even lighting, consistent moisture, and no wind, but as the going gets tougher, so must your plants. Hardening off is the physical process of toughening tender seedlings to outdoor conditions — think of it as boot camp for would-be transplants. By gradually strengthening the cuticle, or outer layer, of stems and foliage, the plants will be much better able to tolerate direct sunlight, wind, and temperature fluctuations.

Begin by setting the potted plants outdoors in a spot protected from wind or harsh sunlight for a little while each day. How long they should stay out depends on your weather, but start with an hour on the first day. Put the seedlings in a protected spot where they will receive bright light but not direct sun. Lengthen the duration a couple of hours each day, making sure to bring them in at night.

After about a week of adjustment, your tender seedlings should be tough enough to survive in the garden. Water them thoroughly before you transplant them and, if possible, do your planting on a cool, overcast day, not a sunny one. If you must plant on a bright, hot day, provide some shade with bushel baskets, sheets, or pieces of lattice propped on supports — anything that will protect small plants from a harsh adjustment.

Until nighttime temperatures are consistently over 50°F (10°C), be prepared to protect seedlings at night with hot caps, plastic milk jugs (cut off the bottoms), or a plastic row cover. You can also place a commercially produced Wall o' Water over each transplant as soon as it goes into the ground. These are connected plastic tubes that are filled with water as insulation. The water warms during the day and releases warmth to the plants overnight.

Resources for Gardeners

{ INCLUDING TONS OF WEBSITES }

COOPERATIVE EXTENSION SERVICE OFFICE

Each state has a Land Grant University under which the Cooperative Extension Service is organized. To find an office in your area, look in your phone book under "[Your] County Government." It may also be listed in regular listings as "Cooperative Extension Service." The staff is a great source of advice on many gardening and food preservation topics. They can give you materials, advice, and information for programs on becoming a Master Gardener, preserving food, composting and more. You can also find them by contacting:

COOPERATIVE STATE RESEARCH, EDUCATION, AND EXTENSION SERVICE

National Institute of Food and Agriculture
Washington, D.C.
202-720-4423
www.csrees.usda.gov/Extension

GARDENING TIPS AND INFORMATION

ALL-AMERICAN SELECTIONS
630-963-0770
www.all-americaselections.org
You can view the complete list of winners since 1933.

NATIONAL GARDENING ASSOCIATION
802-863-5251
www.garden.org
Lots of general gardening help

ORGANIC GARDENING MAGAZINE
800-666-2206
www.organicgardening.com

SEEDS OF CHANGE
888-762-7333
www.seedsofchange.com
Seeds and growing information

SQUARE FOOT GARDENING FOUNDATION
info@squarefootgardening.com
www.squarefootgardening.com

THOMPSON & MORGAN
800-274-7333
www.tmseeds.com
The company's website contains its catalog plus lots of gardening information.

THE UNITED STATES NATIONAL ARBORETUM
www.usna.usda.gov/Hardzone
USDA Plant Hardiness Zone Map

USEFUL PLANTS NURSERY
828-699-6517
www.usefulplants.org

VEGETABLE MD ONLINE
Cornell University, Department of Plant Pathology
http://vegetablemdonline.ppath.cornell.edu/Tables/TableList.htm
A complete list of disease-resistant vegetable varieties, including specific disease resistances

YANKEE GARDENER
www.yankeegardener.com
Seeds, recipes, gardening information, and newsletter

Composting and Mulching Information

COMMUNITY COMPOSTING
Contact your local solid-waste-management agency for information on projects in your area. They may be listed in the phone book under city or town government. If you have trouble locating the right agency, call your county's Cooperative Extension Service.

COMPOSTING
Eartheasy
888-451-6752
www.eartheasy.com/grow_compost.html

COMPOSTING FACT SHEETS
Cornell Waste Management Institute
http://cwmi.css.cornell.edu/factsheets.htm

MULCHING
Natural Resources Conservation Service
www.nrcs.usda.gov/feature/backyard/Mulching.html

Gardening Forums Online
Join in and get your gardening questions answered for free.

FORUMGARDEN.COM
www.forumgarden.com
Lots of general gardening help

GARDEN FORUMS
GardenGuides.com
http://my.gardenguides.com/forums
Lots of general gardening help

GARDENING WITH THE HELPFUL GARDENER
www.helpfulgardener.com

GARDENWEB FORUMS
http://forums.gardenweb.com/forums
Gardeners helping gardeners on tons of topics. Scroll down to Vertical Gardening for specific up-to-the-minute help.

WEBSITES TO VISIT

AEROFALLS

Perception Development Company

www.aerofalls.com

EASIEST GARDEN

www.easiestgarden.com

Hydroponic vertical pipe system and 3-D barrel gardening

ELT EASY GREEN

www.eltlivingwalls.com

Makers of the Living Wall and Green Roof systems

GREEN LIVING TECHONOLOGIES, LLC

http://agreenroof.com

Commercial installation of green roofs and walls

PLANTSONWALLS.COM

www.plantsonwalls.com

Makers of mini-pocket panels and full-pocket panels made from 100% non-toxic recycled plastic bottles

WOOLY POCKET GARDEN COMPANY, INC.

www.woollypockets.com

Recycled plastic bottles, felted and made into special pockets to hang on your wall and fill with plants

For Inspiration

FLOWER WINDOW BOXES

www.flowerwindowboxes.com

Directions on how to install window boxes

THE VERTICAL FARM

www.verticalfarm.com

VERTICAL FARMING

Farm Philly

http://farmphilly.com/group/vertical-farming

Great concept site for modular grow boxes

VERTICAL GARDEN INSTITUTE

http://verticalgardeninstitute.org

Started by Phil Yates, of Oregon City, Oregon, in July 2010, the Vertical Garden Institute is a start-up nonprofit organization dedicated to promoting vertical gardens through sales of vertical gardens and related items, research, education, and fostering vertical garden partnerships throughout the world.

THE WINDOW FARMS PROJECT

www.windowfarm.org

Urban indoor hydroponic window gardening

GARDENING SUPPLIES AND NURSERIES

CATALOGMONSTER

www.catalogmonster.com

Click on Gardening Supplies for several pages of free catalog offers.

FISKARS

www.fiskars.com

After choosing your country, look under "Products" and click on "Yard and Garden" for a selection of well-made products, including rain barrels.

FREE GARDENING CATALOGS

Monteran Outdoor Tips

www.monteran.com/outdoors/catalogs.html

GARDEN HARVEST SUPPLY
888-907-4769
www.gardenharvestsupply.com

GEMPLER'S
GHC Specialty Brands, LLC
800-382-8473
www.gemplers.com

HENRY FIELD'S SEED & NURSERY CO.
513-354-1495
www.henryfields.com

NATURE HILLS NURSERY, INC.
888-864-7663
www.naturehills.com

PLANET NATURAL
800-289-6656
www.planetnatural.com

SMITH & HAWKEN
Target
800-591-3869
www.target.com/smithandhawken

SPRING HILL NURSERIES
Gardens Alive, Inc.
513-354-1510
www.springhillnursery.com

W. ATLEE BURPEE & CO.
800-333-5808
www.burpee.com

SEEDS AND PLANTING INFORMATION

INTERNATIONAL SEED SAVING INSTITUTE
www.seedsave.org

PARK SEED CO.
800-845-3369
www.parkseed.com

ORGANIC SEED PARTNERSHIP
www.plbr.cornell.edu/psi

SEED SAVERS EXCHANGE
563-382-5990
www.seedsavers.org
Seeds and vegetable planting and seed saving instructions

TERRITORIAL SEED COMPANY
800-626-0866
www.territorialseed.com

Trellises and Supports

BESTNEST.COM
877-562-1818
www.bestnest.com

EXTERIOR ACCENTS
888-784-6461
http://exterior-accents.com

FREE TRELLIS PLANS
FreeWW.com
www.freeww.com/trellis.html
Directions on how to build various trellises

GARDEN WINDS
877-479-4637
www.gardenwinds.com

GARDENER'S SUPPLY COMPANY
888-833-1412
www.gardeners.com

G.I. DESIGNS
877-442-6773
www.gidesigns.net

SIMPLYARBORS.COM
Hayneedle Inc.
866-579-5182
www.simplyarbors.com

SIMPLYTRELLISES.COM
Hayneedle Inc.
www.simplytrellises.com

STOCKYARDS RANCH SUPPLY INC.
303-287-8081
www.stockyardsupply.com
Materials to make your own trellises

THE TRELLIS STORE
888-924-3946
http://thetrellisstore.com

WOODLANDDIRECT
800-919-1904
www.woodlanddirect.com

Products to Try

3-D BARREL GARDENS
Easiest Garden
www.easiestgarden.com

AEROFALLS
Perception Development Company
info@aerofalls.com
www.percdev.com
Aeroponic growing systems

GARDEN SUPPLY INC.
888-978-4769
www.stack-a-pots.com
Freestanding and hanging stackable
planter systems

MODULAR INTERLOCKING LIVING WALL SYSTEMS
ELT Easy Green
www.eltlivingwalls.com

PLANTSONWALLS.COM
www.plantsonwalls.com
Mini-pocket panels and full pocket panels

THE VERTICAL GARDEN
877-775-4769
www.theverticalgarden.com
Stackable growing containers

WINDOW FARMS
The Window Farms Project
www.windowfarm.org

WOOLLY POCKETS
Woolly Pocket Garden Company, Inc.
www.woollypockets.com

INDEX

Page numbers in *italic* indicate illustrations;
those in **bold** indicate charts.

A

A-frame
  bed design, 5, *5*, 84, *84*
  construction of, *27*, 27–28
  swing set as, 54, *54*
  thinking outside the, 16
  trellis, 12, *12*
annual vines. *See* vines
apple trees for espalier, 141–44
  basics, 143–44
  designs, *139*
  varieties, 142–43
apricot trees for espalier, 147–49
arches and arbors, 28, *28*, 71, *71*, *126*
  practical considerations, 30

B

bags and totes, 37, *37*
bamboo
  for framework, 14, *14*
  for support system, 16
barrels, 44–45, *45*
basics, vertical gardening, 1–10, *5*
  crop yields, 5–6
  light and air, 4–5
  pests, 5
  rules to grow by, 6–10, *7*
  shaded spots, 4
  space maximization, 2–4
  upkeep, 4
baskets
  hanging, *38*, 38–39
  wire mesh, 40, 42, *42*
beans, 48–55, *50*, *51*
  planting guidelines, 53–54
  site/soil requirements, 52–53
  support system for, 20, *20*
  training to grow up, *54*, 54–55
  varieties, 48–52
blackberries, 104–9
  planting guidelines, 108
  pruning pointers, 109, *109*
  site/soil requirements, 107–8
  training to grow up, *108*, 108–9
  varieties, 104–7, *105*
building materials, 11–18
  containers, 18
  for framework, 11–14, *12*, *13*
  for support system, 14–18, *15*

C

cages, 26–27, 70, *70*
chemicals to avoid, 12
cinder blocks, 41, *41*
clips. *See* ties/clips/slings
clothesline trellis, *25*, 25–26
composting
  basics, 8
  information sources, 159
containers. *See also* pots and planters
  bags and totes, 37, *37*
  creativity in using, 18
  planting recommendations, **32**
  self-watering, 7, *7*
  with trellises, 24, *24*
  in window boxes, 34, 36
Cooperative Extension Service, 158
corn, 55, *55*
cucumbers, *72*, 72–77, *73*, *74*
  burpless, story behind, 75
  planting guidelines, 75–76
  secret life of, 77
  site/soil requirements, 74
  training to grow up, 76, *76*
  transplanting, 39
  varieties, 72–74

D

direct seeding, 154

dirt. *See* soil

drainage, 33

drupe, 105

E

espalier, 138–50

    apple trees, *139*, 141–44

    apricots/peaches/nectarines, 147–49

    basic designs, 138–41, *139*

    pear trees, 144–47

    plum trees, 149–50

    tree selection, 141

F

fences, as trellises, 25–26

    clothesline trellis, *25*, 25–26

    fruits growing on, 96, *96*

    vegetables growing on, 52, *52*, 102, *102*

framework, building, 11–14

    bamboo, 14, *14*

    metal, 13, *13*

    plastic, 14

    wood, *12*, 12–13

fruits, perennial, 103. *See also* espalier; specific
    fruit

future vertical projects, 45

G

gardening

    products to try, 162

    supplies/nurseries, 160–61

gardening tips/information, 158–59

    composting/mulching, 159

    online gardening forums, 159

gherkins, 73

gourds. *See* squash

grapes, 122–31, *124*

    edible leaves of, 129

    planting guidelines, 127–28

    pruning tips, 130–31

    site/soil requirements, 126–27

    thinning out leaves/fruit, 128

    training to grow up, *126*, 128–30, *130*

    varieties, 123–26

greens, 22, 44

H

hanging baskets, *38*, 38–39, *69*, *119*

hardening off transplants, 157

height of plants, 3, *3*

herbs grown in 'bags,' 37, *37*

hybrid support system, 29, *29*

I

irrigation. *See* water/watering

K

kiwis, 132–37

    male/female plants, 134

    planting guidelines, 135

    pruning, 136

    site/soil requirements, 134–35

    training to grow up, *135*, 135–37

    varieties, 132–34

L

landscape blocks, 41, *41*

living wall, creating a, 46, *46*

M

Malabar spinach (*Basella alba*), 22

materials. *See* building materials

melons, 86–96, *87*, *88*, *89*, *92*

    out of the ordinary, 91

    planting guidelines, 94–95

    secret life of, 93

    seedless seeds, treatment for, 95

    site/soil requirements, 94

    training to grow up, *94*, 96, *96*

    varieties, 86–94

mesh and wire, 15–16
metal
    cages, 13, *13*, 70, *70*
    galvanized/nongalvanized, 16
    spiraling stake, 26, *26*
    for towers, 43, *43*
mulch/mulching
    basics, 9
    information sources, 159

N
nectarine trees for espalier, 147–49

O
online gardening forums, 159
organic produce, 3

P
peach trees for espalier, 147–49
pear trees for espalier, 144–47
    Asian pears, 145–46
    basics, 146–47
    European pears, 144–45
    varieties, 144
peas, 56–60, *57, 58, 60*
    planting guidelines, 59–60
    site/soil requirements, 59
    support system for, 20, *20*
    training to grow up, 60, *60*
    varieties, 56–58
pests, checking for, 5
planters. *See* pots and planters
plastic pipe. *See* PVC pipe
plum trees for espalier, 149–50
potatoes. *See* sweet potatoes
pots and planters, 38–42. *See also* containers
    creativity in using, 41, *41*
    hanging baskets, *38*, 38–39
    modular planters, 46, *46*
    strawberry pots, 121, *121*
    upside-down, *39*, 39–40, 42

produce, organic, 3
pumpkins. *See* squash
PVC pipe, 14
PVC spacer, 7, *7*

R
raised beds
    A-frame with, 5, *5*
    basics, 8
    multilevel, 41, *41*
raspberries, 110–16, *111*, 115–16
    planting guidelines, 114–15
    pruning tips, 116
    relocation of patch, 115
    site/soil requirements, 114
    training to grow up, *115*, 115–16
    varieties, 110–13
recordkeeping, 10
roots, making room for, 32–33
rope/twine/string, 14–15
rotating crops, 10
rules to grow by, 6–10, *7*
    composting, 8
    mulching, 9
    raised beds, 8
    rotating crops, 10
    staking/supporting plants, 9
    sunlight, 6
    watering wisely, 6–10
    weeding, 9–10

S
salad bar, vertical, 44
seedlings, growing, 155–56
seeds/seeding
    direct seeding, 154
    and planting information, 161–62
    saving seeds, 4
self-watering containers, 7, *7*
shade, 4, 31–32, **32**
shelves for plants, 41, *41*

slings, *82*, *96*
    setting up, 17–18, *18*
    ties, clips and, 16–18, *17*, **17**
    for very large fruit, 83
soil
    considerations, 3–4
    depth, **32**
    sterile growing medium, 34
    weight of, 38
space-saving options, 31–46
    bags and totes, 37, *37*
    containers, **32**
    preliminaries, 31–33
    window boxes, *33*, 33–34, 36, *36*
    window farming, 35, *35*
spacing of plants, **32**
spinach
    Malabar spinach (*Basella alba*), 22
squash, *55*, 78–85, *79*, *80*
    planting guidelines, 83–84
    site/soil requirements, 83
    support system for, 21, *21*
    training to grow up, *82*, 82, *84*, 84–85, *85*
    transplanting, 39
    varieties, 78–83
staking/supporting plants, 9
    basics, 19–20
    length of stakes, 21
    spiraling metal stake, 26, *26*
strawberries, *117*, 117–22, *122*
    in containers, *119*, *121*, 121, *122*
    planting guidelines, 120
    site/soil requirements, 120
    training to grow up, 120, 122
    varieties, 118–20
    strawberry pots, 121, *121*
string/rope/twine, 14–15
sun/sunlight, **32**
    air and, 4–5
    direction of, 3, *3*
    hours per day, 6

    shade and, 31–32
support system design, 14–18, *15*
    ties/clips/slings, 16–18, *17*, **17**
    twine/string/rope, 14–15
    wire and mesh, 15–16, 26–27, *27*
    wood and bamboo, 16
support systems, sources for, 161–62
support systems, traditional, 19. *See also* arches
    and arbors; tepees; trellises
sweet potatoes, 97–102, *98*
    nutritional benefits, 101
    planting guidelines, *100*, 100–101
    site/soil requirements, 99
    tater tower, building, 42–43, *43*
    training to grow up, 102, *102*
    varieties, 97–99

T
    tater tower, building, 42–43, *43*
tepees, *20*, *21*
    four-legged, 23
    with horizontal rungs, 24, *24*
    large, 21, 23
    running, 23, *23*
    small, 20–21
    vegetables growing on, 21, *21*, 50, *50*, 85, *85*
Three Sisters Garden, 55, *55*
ties/clips/slings, 16–18, *17*, **17**
tomatillos, 67
tomatoes, 61–71
    classification of, 61
    in containers, 69, *69*
    disease resistance of, 63
    grown in 'bags,' 37, *37*
    nutritional benefits, 67
    planting guidelines, 68–70
    root systems of, 33
    site/soil requirements, 67–68
    for stuffing, 65
    support systems for, 27, *27*, *29*, *70*, 70–71, *71*
    training to grow up, 70–71, *71*

in upside-down planters, 39, *39*

varieties, 62–67

towers/towering, 42–45

   barrels used in, 44–45, *45*

   tater tower, building, 42–43, *43*

transplants, hardening off, 157

trellises

   design options, 6

   fences as, *25*, 25–26

   ready-made, 13

   self-contained, 24, *24*

   sources for, 161–62

   storage of, 12

   V-shaped, 115, *115*

tuteurs, 13, 24, *24*

twine/string/rope, 14–15

U

upside-down planters, *39*, 39–40, 42

USDA hardiness zone map, *153*

V

varieties, recommended, 151–52

vines

   annual, 47. *See also* specific plant

   hybrid support system for, 29, *29*

   training, 9

   tying too tight, 17

   wet, avoiding touching, 8

W

wall, living, 46, *46*

water/watering, 6–7

   aqua spikes, *7*

   drip irrigation, *7*

   homemade irrigation system, 7, *7*

   self-watering containers, 7, *7*

   wet vines and, 8

websites, 160

weeding, 9–10

window boxes, *33*, 33–36

building materials, 33–34

   containers in, 34, 36

   creativity in using, 36, *36*

window farming, 35, *35*

wire and mesh, 15–16

   cool cages from, 26–27, *27*

   wire mesh baskets, 40, 42, *42*

wood

   cages, 26–27

   for framework, 12, *12*, 43, *43*

   for support system, 16

   treated, chemicals in, 12

Z

zone map, *153*

Other Storey Titles You Will Enjoy

Carrots Love Tomatoes, by **Louise Riotte.**
A classic companion planting guide that shows how to use plants' natural partnerships to produce bigger and better harvests.
224 pages. Paper. ISBN 978-1-58017-027-7.

Growing Chinese Vegetables in Your Own Backyard, by **Geri Harrington.**
Plant-by-plant advice on choosing, planting, growing, harvesting, and cooking more than 40 Chinese vegetables and herbs.
232 pages. Paper. ISBN 978-1-60342-140-9.

Landscaping with Fruit, by **Lee Reich.**
A complete, accessible guide to luscious landscaping — from alpine strawberry to lingonberry, mulberry to wintergreen.
192 pages. Paper. ISBN 978-1-60342-091-4.
Hardcover with jacket. ISBN 978-1-60342-096-9.

Starter Vegetable Gardens, by **Barbara Pleasant.**
A great resource for beginning vegetable gardeners: 24 no-fail plans for small organic gardens.
180 pages. Paper. ISBN 978-1-60342-529-2.

The Veggie Gardener's Answer Book, by **Barbara W. Ellis.**
Insider's tips and tricks, practical advice, and organic wisdom for vegetable growers everywhere.
432 pages. Flexibind. ISBN 978-1-60342-024-2.

Week-by-Week Vegetable Gardener's Handbook, by **Ron Kujawski & Jennifer Kujawski.**
Detailed, customizable to-do lists to break down gardening into simple, manageable tasks.
200 pages. Paper. ISBN 978-1-60342-694-7.

These and other books from Storey Publishing are available wherever quality books are sold or by calling 1-800-441-5700.
Visit us at *www.storey.com*.